Fly Fishing the Baja and Beyond:

A Guide's Perspective on Fly Fishing for Roosterfish and Other Tropical Pacific Species

by Mike Rieser

Fly Fishing the Baja and Beyond

by Mike Rieser

Published by:
Baja Time Publications

Copyright 2010 Mike Rieser, Baja Time Publications
Printed in the United States of America
ISBN 978-0-578-07556-3

Art and layout by Robin Meetz and Dina Carson; Imagination Technology Corporation, www.imaginationtechnology.com

Cover photo by Brian O'Keefe. Interior photos by Brian O'Keefe, Eric Kummerfeldt, Adam Graham and the author.

Mike Rieser is available for seminars and workshops related to the material of this book and may be contacted by email at bajamikefish@yahoo.com

To order online, please go to www.lulu.com, www. amazon.com or other online book retailers.

Table of Contents

Photograph by Brian O'Keefe

Acknowledgments

In writing this book I am indebted to Larry Henderson, my original business partner, for his insight and uncanny ability to catch fish in fresh or saltwater. Partners John Matson and Bob Dettmann continually provided fresh insight and new approaches to saltwater fly fishing. Our valuable guides, past and present, have years of experience and deserve a tremendous amount of credit for many of the ideas expressed in this book.

This book and our guide business would not exist were it not for the Van Wormer Family. Robert Van Wormer built Hotel Punta Colorada in 1964 as one of the early-day fishing resorts on the East Cape, a family tradition that continues to this day. The Van Wormers have been at the forefront of conserving the resources of the Sea of Cortez serving as a role model for the rest of Mexico as well as other Central American countries. It was their vision to engage the fly fishing community as a means to bring more conservation-minded fishermen to the Sea of Cortez. I am fortunate to be included in their dream.

Last, but certainly not least, so much credit goes to the Mexican Captains with whom I spend my days on the Sea of Cortez, and quite often my evenings as well. For generations they have lived "en los brazos del Mar (in the arms of the sea).

My very first ventures off shore were with the gypsy Pangueros, who moved from one remote camp to another, plying their trade in wooden boats called Pangas. They hauled their catch with hand lines and truly lived by the mercy of the sea. They knew nothing of the fly rod, but were quite willing to share their knowledge of the Sea of Cortez. I suspect that our fishing efforts with the wimpy rod were a great entertainment to our gracious hosts. Today's sport fishing Captains trace their origins back through many generations of such fishermen. We continue to learn from them, while still providing plenty of entertainment along the way.

Photograph by Brian O'Keefe

1

Origins:
Climbing on the
Learning Curve

The rusty old tackle box lay half buried in sand on the leeward side of the Pismo sand dunes. We had taken shelter from the ceaseless spring winds along the shores of Oso Flaco Lake when we discovered it. The pounding Pacific surf mixed with the calls of grebes, mud hens and redwing black birds as my father circled the tackle box looking for tracks or other signs of ownership. My eyes locked onto this treasure trove and waited on my father's word that we could go ahead and open it. We were on a family picnic. I was five and already a confirmed fisherman. The mere fact that I had yet to catch anything only fired the furnace of my imagination. Little did I know the many ripples that would flow from this small event, shaping the shorelines of my fishing life.

"It appears this tackle box has been here some time. I don't think that anyone will be back to claim it," declared my father. With these words my fantasies of fishing treasure exploded, only to be temporarily dashed when my father continued. "It's best we leave it here 'till the end of the day and see if any one returns for it." For the duration of our picnic, my attention never left that rusty old box. At last my father said, "It's time we have a look."

Aged with rust, the tackle box resisted our initial efforts to open it, finally yielding to the pressure of my Dad's pocket knife. At first I was disappointed in its contents. Most of the hooks were rusted beyond use. A few battered bass plugs, leader material, some bobbers and a fish stringer were about all that occupied the top trays of the box. Another container lay within the lower portion of the box and I waited in eager anticipation as my father opened it, to reveal its hidden treasure. I wasn't sure what to make of the funny looking reel with its thick fishing line, nor the small fuzzy fluffs on hooks wrapped in a soft leather pouch. "Fly fishing stuff," my father observed.

Several picnics later, alongside a substantial hole on the Santa Ynez River, I insisted that we bring our rods and the rusty tackle box on the chance we would encounter fish. Sure enough, a school of blue gills appeared around a submerged log across from our picnic site. I could barely contain my excitement at this discovery. I fidgeted and twitched all through lunch. Since fishing was not the purpose of the trip, we had not brought bait with us. My father attached one of the flies to a leader behind one of the bobbers and cast the rig in the general direction of the bluegill without much confidence. The image of what happened next is as fresh today as the day it happened. A bluegill slid out from behind the log and slurped in the little fly. I have not been the same since.

It is no coincidence that the tackle box contained both fresh and saltwater gear along with the handful of flies and the old fly reel. I grew to love fishing the Pacific Ocean, first with conventional gear, then eventually with fly tackle. I also developed a fascination for fly fishing all manner of fresh water species. Experience gained in one aspect of fishing lent itself to applications in the others. As a theme in this book, you will find many cross references to lessons learned from fishing live bait on conventional gear to fishing trout, steelhead and striped bass on the fly.

My expanding world of fishing eventually led to the Baja in 1974 where I became entranced by the landscape, the people, and the Sea of Cortez's incredible fishery. During my early Baja years, I worked summer and fall for an outfitter guide service and eventually as a seasonal employee for the United States Forest Service. Thus, my winters were free to explore the richness of the Sea of Cortez. Little was written at that time on saltwater fly fishing outside of the growing interest in tarpon and bonefish on the flats. Fly fishing for stripers along the East and West Coasts was becoming popular, a pursuit I had enjoyed while in school in the Bay Area. To meet the challenge of being a fly fishing "pioneer" in the Sea of Cortez, I pulled from the scarce literature, my fresh water fly fishing knowledge and my saltwater conventional experience. What followed was a long and often steep learning curve, one that I am still climbing, while gaining new insights with each fishing season.

The lessons learned fishing the Sea of Cortez can and have been applied to other areas of the tropical Pacific. The techniques that we use to catch dorado, roosterfish, billfish and tuna work just as well in Guatemala, Costa Rica, Southern California and other parts of Mexico. It is a happy circumstance that the Sea of Cortez is out my front door and where I ply my trade as a fly fishing guide at the Van Wormer Resorts. I have learned a great deal from my own fishing and from the shared experience of fishing with partners, guides and friends.

When it comes to observing fish behavior and response to various techniques, nothing quite equals the experience of guiding clients. As a guide, I am not directly involved in making the cast, delivering the proper presentation, nor the multitude of other distractions that can pull focus away from what the fish is doing. I learned this lesson years ago guiding trout fishermen and found that I saw subtleties with the drift of a strike indicator that I tended not to see when I actually fished. It is simply a different perspective. That, coupled with my own fishing experience, has provided a broader approach to writing this book.

I write this book primarily from the perspective of guide and to a degree from the fisherman inside me. The intent is not to write a book on how to guide, although earlier drafts have been found useful by the guides that work for us and I am sure that other guides will look at this book and compare their own experiences. It is really a book about putting pieces of the puzzle together to catch salt water fish. I borrow greatly from the vast collective experience, my own and many others, in trout fishing that focuses on fish behavior relative to the response to their environment, and the available food source.

Saltwater species also display certain identifiable behavioral characteristics when they encounter a potential food source, be it the scaled and slimy mullet, or an imitation dressed in hair and feathers. For me, the observation of feeding behavior in its various stages is the beginning of piecing together an approach to selecting the manner of teasing, the fly and the retrieve. Sometimes the solutions are obvious, such as encountering vast boils of feeding fish. In extreme feeding behavior, the choice of fly or technique is moot. About anything will work. But, does this teach us much more than when the fish are really hungry they will eat any fly on any retrieve? Actually, the converse may be true. Many folks stop at this point well satisfied that they have the right fly and the right strip cadence, and continue to fish that species regardless of the fish behavior displayed. It is easy to get pulled into this approach when you base all your experience on a small snap shot in time. This was true for me when I first visited the Baja as a fisherman and to an extent when I travel some place new for species unfamiliar to me. From my earliest experiences, the feeding frenzies were easy; the rest was a mystery when the techniques I had developed failed under other circumstances. With enough time on the water, patterns began to emerge. The focus became sharper with more time observing clients fishing and fish reacting. The learning curve began to flatten out.

Developing an ability to better read the fish, greatly increases the catch rate. The concept sounds simple enough if you can get past the bias and gratification that comes from the occasional encounter of the easy fish, or the fish that follows the fly and refuses at the last second. This applies to dorado and jack crevalle as much as it does to roosterfish. The former two considered easy, the latter very difficult. Despite all that has been written and said about how easy dorado are to catch on the fly, spend enough time on the water and you will encounter plenty of persnickety fish that will ignore pre-programmed tactics reinforced by previously encountered easy fish. These tough fish may be catchable if you can read their behavior and adjust accordingly.

Roosterfish are normally a challenge to catch on the fly. Hell, many times they are a challenge to catch on live bait. But they, like all predators, go on feeding binges and respond well to a range of flies and retrieves. A pause in the strip, slower cadence or even a dead drop will occasionally work when the fish are really aggressive. Take that small snap shot and apply it to all the roosterfish encounters that follow and it might be a long time before you catch your next fish. Roosterfish and other species reinforce our misleading approaches by giving a follow to the fly, but refusing at the last second, leaving us with the mistaken impression that our techniques are appropriate.

Happily the techniques that work for the tough dorado or even tougher roosterfish are highly effective for the easy fish. The content of this book focuses a lot of attention on roosterfish as an example of relating fish feeding behavior to tactical approaches. By using techniques that work for the toughest fish under normal conditions, you will more than cover the easy situations. There are fish that are uncatchable and it's a better use of time and energy to search out the responsive fish. Again, recognizing and understanding feeding behavior is the beginning point to catching more fish.

Along the way there are chapters on the tackle, leaders, knots and fish fighting techniques. These fundamentals form a foundation intended to improve the odds of success, once the fish of a lifetime is on the hook.

Photograph by Brian O'Keefe

Photograph by Brian O'Keefe

2

The Gear:
What's in Your Wallet?

Fly tackle has come a long way since my first adventures on the Baja. During those early years I fished with what I could afford, which wasn't much considering that I worked as a seasonal employee of the United States Forest Service and fall season fishing guide. Likewise, the selection of tackle at that time was almost as limited as my budget. The Phlueger Medalist reels that served me well for salmon and steelhead went through some hellish product testing on tuna, dorado, jacks, billfish and other such bruisers. I caught fish by day and fixed reels by Coleman lantern at night. The Fenwick glass rods of that era performed rather well, and I am glad to see a return to fiberglass as a rod-building component for big game fly rods.

Times have changed, the selection of tackle today is mind boggling with as many options as a Cabo time share salesman has opening lines. As you might expect, the price range is as varied as the number of options. My advice is to not let the price of tackle deter you from entering the world of saltwater fly fishing. Much of the tackle available today is of a quality to the task while not necessarily devastating to the wallet.

Reels

From this working guide's perspective, a fly reel doesn't have to exceed the price of the airline ticket that gets you to the fishing. That being said, there are some very high quality, but pricy reels, that work with the precision of a Swiss watch. There is definitely something to be said about the pride of ownership of a very fine reel. I have acquired a few along the way and I do find joy in listening to them purr when I spin their cranks. There is an adage out there that one should buy the best reel one can afford. That cliché may have been true in the days of my early explorations of the Baja, the Phlueger being the best I could afford at that time. Today, the quality of many of the moderate priced reels is more than adequate to the purpose and the move to an expensive reel, in my mind, becomes more a matter of esthetics, regardless of your economic means.

Fly reels designed for the salt come in a variety of basic designs: direct drives, anti-reverse, large arbor and standard. It gets more complicated after you break down the basic categories.

Direct Drive Reels

Let's look at direct drive versus anti-reverse. By direct drive we mean that for every turn of the reel handle the arbor turns the same number of revolutions or a 1:1 rate of retrieve.

Direct drive reels are simple machines that give you a 1:1 ratio of retrieve. For each turn of the reel handle, the spool turns once. The advantage is less cost, fewer moving parts to fail, less weight and near infinite control on the fish. With a direct drive reel, you have the ability to make instantaneous adjustments to the drag tension by palming the rim of the spool. Control of the fish at boat side is directly related to the pressure applied or released. This adjustment takes place much quicker with direct drive reels, allowing you to either take quick advantage of a tired fish, or to instantly back off a fish that explodes away from the boat and eminent capture. Remember, we use very light leaders with fly tackle and the margin of error on the side of pressuring big fish at the boat is very small.

We choose direct drive reels for our guide business. Given the relatively light tippets, we try to protect them from breaking by setting our drags within the range of four to six pounds of pressure then leave them alone for the duration of the fight. All changes of pressure to the fish are applied by palm pressure to the rim or pinching the fly line to the cork handle. In the chapter on fighting fish we will discuss this topic in more detail.

Anti-Reverse Reels

An anti-reverse reel works much like a conventional level wind reel, in that the spool or arbor will slip when a fish is running via a drag system. Many of the anti-reverse reels also have a set of gears that multiply the revolutions of the arbor or spool for each turn of the crank handle. The advantage to these reels is that the spool turns while the crank handle does not, thus eliminating the chance of getting your knuckles banged when a good fish blitzes for the horizon. These reels have the advantage of gaining more line per revolution of the reel handle than a direct drive. These reels work well for the angler who prefers to play their fish by applying pressure through adjustment of the drag system. The disadvantages are higher cost, additional weight and ability to make quick pressure adjustments to the fish at boat side. Since these reels are not built for palming the rim, all pressure adjustments on the fish are made by drag control. At boat side, the angle can over tighten the drag only to break the fish away if it makes a sudden surge before the angler can back off the drag control knob.

Large Arbor vs. Standard Arbor Reels

The second basic consideration is a choice between large arbor reels versus a standard arbor. A few years ago this discussion was more relevant than today when the large arbor revolution was just getting started. The point is almost moot now that most reels designed for saltwater big game come in large arbor configurations.

Choosing a Good Saltwater Reel

So, given the multitude of options, here are some of the other qualities I look for in a good saltwater reel, price notwithstanding.

The first consideration is that the reel will stand up to the corrosive effect of saltwater. The best reels are constructed from a solid block of high-quality, aircraft-grade aluminum and are triple anodized to keep the salt from corroding them. Yes, saltwater will corrode aluminum if given enough exposure and scratching of the anodized layer of protection. The toughest reels we have found for scratch and corrosion resistance are constructed of 6061 aircraft-grade aluminum and are type-III, hard anodized.

Protection against corrosion of the inner workings of the reel is of even greater concern than a well-preserved exterior. The best reels have bearings completely sealed from saltwater exposure. If they are not sealed, then they should be easily accessible for cleaning on a regular basis.

In the case of saltwater fly reels, size does matter, both in line capacity and spool diameter as related to its cranking capability. More on cranking in a bit, let's talk capacity first. The size of the reel and its capacity is relative to the target species to a point, barring any of the surprises you might encounter in pursuit of the target species. Beware that Bubba lurks in all the waters of the Sea and you may find yourself quite suddenly hooked up and under gunned.

A friend of ours perched himself a top a large boulder casting his eight weight rod with a small reel, expecting to catch the small green jacks and ladyfish frequenting that part of the beach. He didn't factor in Bubba, who, in this case, was a forty-something pound roosterfish that absolutely annihilated his small Clouser, streaked for the horizon, leaving our friend atop his rock spooled and shaking.

Lesson learned, here's your sign. For shoreline fishing, a good quality salt-water reel should be able to hold 200 yards of either 30 lb. Dacron backing, or 50 lb. Spectra. Our reels used for off-shore fishing are loaded with 300 to 500 yards of backing.

Back to cranking capacity, simply stated we like large arbor reels. Large arbors have a decided advantage over standard arbors as they affect the rate of retrieve. With the 1:1 retrieve ratio found on direct drive reels, a large arbor returns more line to the spool with each rotation of the reel handle. As the fish pulls, backing off a large arbor reel, the actual effective spool diameter shrinks less than with a standard arbor. The advantage in gaining nine inches of line per rotation versus three inches is huge over the long haul, when slugging it out with a tuna or billfish.

I can well remember the day I first laid eyes on a large arbor reel that showed up with one of our clients. He had undergone some surgery for his shoulder and his doctor recommended that he try using the new large arbor reels, claiming that he would put less long-term stress on the repaired shoulder. I was skeptical at first and concerned that the reel would tweak between the frame and spool. I also wondered if the hype about large arbors was just that, hype. It also occurred to me that my friend was using a doctor's excuse to slip the purchase of a new reel past his wife. As it turned out, we experienced some incredible tuna fishing that week with lots of fish hooked and some very tired clients by day's end.

On the fourth day, the client, having had as much fun as his shoulder would allow, handed me the rod and said "land the sucker, I'm taking a break." So I did and, wow, it hit me how much easier it was to gain line on the fish when I could put more line on the reel with each crank. Soon the fish was in the boat and I was feeling no worse for wear. Meanwhile the other client, using our provided standard-arbor reels, was fighting heroically, but gaining only three inches per crank. Shortly thereafter, he too threw in the towel, handed me the rod with my soon-to-be old-fashioned small arbor reel and went to join his friend who had discovered the cooler of beer. The clients cheered and jeered as the fight wore on. The realization of how tough tuna can be was obvious as the sweat poured off my forehead and the line crept itself onto the spool three inches at a time. "Reel, reel, reel, don't let the fish rest!" chorused the two, repeating the mantra I had been giving them for the past four days. Another lesson learned followed by a substantial purchase of large arbor reels.

Another advantage that large arbor reels have, is that drag pressure remains more consistent due to less change is spool diameter.

Loss of line capacity is a trade off in some models of large arbor reels compared to mid- or standard-sized arbor reels. In most cases, the amount of backing is not as big a concern as presented in the sporting print and most of the large arbor reels designed for saltwater big game have plenty of capacity. Don't get me wrong, these fish make spectacular runs that eat lots of line, but usually well within the capacity of the reel designed for the targeted species. Over the years very few fish have come close to spooling a client. One of the few that came close was a six foot long giant needle that peeled 300 yards of backing in a series of spectacular greyhounding leaps. Were it not for the fast reaction of the captain to follow the fish we would have been looking at the bottom of an empty spool.

Given a choice of high capacity versus gaining line quicker onto the reel, I'll take the later. If either capacity or arbor size is of concern, you can offset the situation by using gel-spun backing. We will discuss the merits and negatives of this product a little later on in this chapter in the section devoted to backing.

Last, but certainly not least, is a good drag system. A lot is written about drag systems and drags are an important consideration in selecting a saltwater reel. The drag system does not need the capability to stop a truck, in my opinion, though lots of advertising dollars lead you to believe so. The most important aspect is that the startup spin of the reel is smooth, and then remains consistent through the fight, not changing with loss of line, heat created by drag friction, or by getting wet. There are two schools of thought on the role of the drag system versus rim control in playing big fish and we will get into that debate in the chapter on playing fish.

Simplicity of drag design is important to us in the guide business and should be to those of you lucky enough to experience extended travel. I have had a devil of a time getting into some $600 reels to fix a drag system that suddenly started free spooling due a bit of salt grime or sand. Dropping it into the mail to the manufacture from the Baja is not an option. From my perspective the reel should be bomb proof or field fixable.

Rods

The selection of saltwater rods equals the multitude of options presented by saltwater reels with many fine products to choose from. As with buying a reel you can spend anywhere from reasonable to some major coin on a rod. The hype in rod advertising, is the ability of the rod to cast beyond the horizon with a loop tighter than a bull's butt in fly season.

The high end rods are wonderful casting tools for the most part and I own and fish a goodly number of them. We also have found some great moderately-priced rods that cast well and stand up to the rigors of playing tough fish. Redington, Temple Fork and St. Croix have started a small revolution in the rod industry by producing moderately-priced rods that cast beautifully and don't shatter into a rain of graphite when pressed by a big fish and amplified by angler error.

Graphite has dominated the rod manufacturing world for about thirty years now with some advances in titanium and boron fibers added to the mix. Graphite is light weight and lends itself extremely well to the faster action casting tools preferred today. Graphite rods, when properly constructed and properly used, will also tolerate a high degree of bend while fighting fish. Each year the designs improve in terms of hoop strength, while retaining a light feel. The draw back in using graphite for blue water fly fishing is that graphite is brittle and subject to breaking in the event of a nick after a collision with a leaded fly, or less than stellar fish fighting technique.

The Temple Fork Company has introduced a new line of rods in their Blue Water series that incorporate fiberglass into the butt section of the rod. Given the brittle nature of graphite, we applaud the move back to fiberglass for heavy lifting. Do these rods give up something in turn of casting characteristics? Yes, to a degree they do. The difference being more apparent to newcomers to saltwater if the heaviest rod they may have thrown prior was a 5 weight. We have a lot of clients who fall into this category and they all seem to adjust to the weight and feel of the bigger rods.

Temple Fork Outfitters has recently introduced an eight foot rod, the Mini Mag, that is big fish tough, handy in tight quarters on the boat and light in the hand.

Saltwater rods tend to fall into two groups, those designed for lifting and those designed for casting and each has its application. In choosing a rod weight and design there are a number of aspects to consider, such as what species do you intend to target, how far do you intend to cast, how much casting during the day will you do compared to how long you will spend fighting fish.

Saltwater Rods Built for Casting

So how far do you really need to cast a fly to catch fish in the Sea of Cortez and the Pacific beyond? Not as far as you might think, the exception being fishing roosterfish from the beach. Most of the shots at the blue water species are usually 40 feet or less. With the sinking lines and bigger flies we throw, the line loops tend to be bigger too. We catch a lot of dorado, roosters and skipjack with a 20 or 30-foot roll cast. Speed and accuracy of delivery out fishes the ability to throw the length of a fly line any day.

My advice is pick a rod with good casting characteristics in the 8-9-10 weight range for use on the beach and for the smaller off-shore species such as skipjack and school-sized dorado. When choosing a 12 to 15 weight rod for off-shore, go with a rod built for heavy lifting and fish fighting ability. Tuna immediately comes to mind when I think of heavy lifting. If your intent is to spend more time on shore looking for big roosterfish, where a lot of casting with big flies may occur, then an 11 or 12 weight with good casting characteristics is recommended. Later in this book I will discuss specific tackle recommendation for specific species.

Tropical fish have amazing speed and strength dictating rod selection heavier than what most fresh water anglers would assume, even those folks with salmon fishing experience. Many is the time that one of our anglers has strained against the pull of their first skipjack, thinking the whole time that they are playing big Moe, only to be totally shocked by the smaller-than-expected size of the fish when they finally land it. For the off-shore scene, a nine weight is adequate for school-size dorado, skipjack, or bonito when casting small flies on calm days. So, does this mean the lighter rods are a good first choice for off shore fishing? I wouldn't recommend it given the choices of rods available and how tough light tackle is on both fish and fisherman. The ten through twelve-weight rods are the better all around choice for fishing the blue water, especially when you may encounter the larger bulls and other species. Billfish and big tuna are another matter, and should not be taken lightly in terms of rod size. I opt for the 14 to 16 weight rods built specifically for these species. If you have but one rod to take, excluding billfish/big tuna, I would go with either a 12 weight or the new Temple Fork Outfitters Blue Water Light.

Lines

Here again, the tackle manufactures have done an incredible job of developing specialty lines in a vast array of different styles. I get swallowed up in the choices when preparing our pre-season line orders considering all the new products on the market. Fishing the Sea of Cortez and Pacific Ocean is a bit more complicated than a trip to the flats in terms of the variety of species and conditions. In the case of line selection, if you're a striper or steelhead fisherman, you will find comfort in the type of lines we use, especially when it comes to shooting heads. Line selection considerations include: the ability to with stand tropical heat, take up as little space on the spool as possible, apply to a variety of situations, cast into the wind, handle cross winds and in some cases sink quickly. Let's look at some of the broad categories of fly lines and their pros and cons, starting with sink rate from top to bottom.

Full-Length Floating Line

This is often the line of choice for the flats fisherman and it serves that situation well. Floating lines are the easiest lines to cast if you are new to fly fishing. Most fly rods are designed around throwing a floating line, and perform best with them. The floaters pick up easily off the water and are the easiest to roll cast. Floating lines are the best choice for fishing poppers and turning over large bulky flies. I often keep a rod rigged with a floating line for this purpose.

If you are new to fly fishing or not used to the heavier saltwater tackle, this is a good initial choice. The disadvantages, although not major, are several. Under windy conditions, the floating line has a greater diameter and doesn't push as easily into a head wind. A cross wind into the shoulder is even more problematic, given the tendency of the wind to push the line back into the one doing the casting (and the guide standing beside them). Full length floating lines take up lots of capacity on the reel, giving up about 25 percent over sinking lines. The loss of reel diameter, or cranking capacity, is as consequential as loss of line capacity.

The thicker diameter of the floating line can create a large belly when a fast running fish makes a turn. This greatly increases pressure on the leader and lessens the degree of control on the fish. Billfish and dorado are notorious for making radical changes in direction during the fight, resulting in major line bellies.

The bottom line is, the floater will work in the same situations as the intermediate line, but with some challenges. Beginners will advance their casting techniques quicker with the floating line and we keep several reels loaded with a floater for this purpose. If it is the only line that you have loaded on your reel and are headed to the Baja or Central America, don't sweat it, the floating line will work for you, just not as efficiently as some other choices available.

Intermediate, Full-Length Lines

Intermediate lines are an excellent all around choice. They excel for beach fishing, roosterfish and some off shore applications, such as dorado schooled up around the boat. For most levels of casting skill, the intermediate line presents fewer problems than fast sinking lines in adjusting the casting stroke or the ability to pick the line off the water. Most fishermen learn to roll cast the intermediate line fairly quickly, as well. The intermediate line casts well in moderate head and cross wind situations and turns over bulky flies almost as well as the floating line, especially if you're using a line one size up from the recommended weight of the rod. Loss of backing capacity is much less than with the floating line, and it does not form nearly as large a belly as the floating line.

The main disadvantage of the intermediate line is in the situations where a deep sink is required to reach fish. Most tuna situations, fishing the reefs for snapper, and in-shore species holding in deeper current rips, dictate a line with a faster rate of sink than available with the intermediate line.

Bottom line, the full length intermediate line covers a good 80 percent of the situations we encounter and we put them on most of our reels intended for the 8 through 10 weight rods and the 12 weights used for big roosters and jacks. Our favorite intermediate is the Scientific Angler Mastery Series clear intermediate tarpon/bonefish line. This line has a tough coating that stands up to the occasional brush with the sand on inadvertently low back casts.

Full-Length Sinking Lines

Many of the lines in this category have their origins in the shooting-head setups we used years ago for steelhead and striper fishing. The line manufactures have since integrated the running line into a short sinking head without the loop connection that hinges the line and clicks its way through the guides. The result is a very good all around line for off shore situations.

The advantages are: good casting characteristics in windy conditions, and spool capacity is much greater with a high density sinking line compared to either the intermediate or floating line. Sinking lines can be used for fishing surface situations, if you don't pause before starting the retrieve. At the same time, they can reach 60 feet deep, if needed for those special situations.

The disadvantage to full sink lines is the challenge for some beginning casters. Depending on the action of the rod, a high-density line tends to shock the tip of the rod on the back cast and leads to a deep tailing loop on the forward cast. For beginners, the sinking line is more difficult to pick up or roll cast, especially in moderate surf situations.

Bottom Line

Sinking lines are our choice for most off shore situations, given the casting ability of the client. For those who struggle while trying to pick up or cast a sinking line, the intermediate or floating lines are good alternatives. The full sink line excels for dead drop presentation for tuna and reef species and can turn the trick for ladyfish and jacks when they are working deep along the beach. The sinking lines are very useable for most beach fishing situations. A retrieve started as soon as the fly hits the water will keep the line and fly in tow close to the surface. Our favorite lines are the Scientific Angler Tropic Express and Blue Water Express. Rio and Teeny also offer several excellent choices in sinking lines.

Shooting Heads

These are the lines I started with on the Baja over thirty years ago and were an adaptation from my steelhead and salmon fishing gear. One of the main advantages to shooting heads is their versatility. With one running line on a spool, you can quickly change the short head section via a loop-to-loop connection, to match the current situation from floating to deep sink. Several fly-line manufactures now offer a combination of heads or tips with the purchase of the base running line. The moderately adept craftsmen can build their own shooting heads fairly easily. Other advantages are: the greatest possible line capacity, longest distance gained in casting, and fastest possible rate of sink over other line types.

The drawback to shooting heads is in the casting for some people. There is no back taper in the head to transition with the radically smaller diameter of the running line. This leads to a hinging feel in the line during the transition from the back stroke to the forward stroke. The loop-to-loop connection between the running line and the head creates a clicking sensation as the knot connection slides through the guides; all situations that mitigate with practice.

If you are inclined to build your own shooting heads, there are several options for the running line portion, including monofilament such as amnesia, braided and coated running line similar to the shooting portion on full length lines. The monofilament casts farther due to its small diameter, and allows the head to sink faster while taking up less room on the spool. It also tends to tangle easier than the other two choices. The braided lines are also very small in diameter. It is fairly easy to back braid a loop in the braided line which results in a small connection. Braided lines are abrasive to the hand while stripping and require the use of a glove to prevent cuts. They are not as prone to tangle as monofilament, but when they do, they are difficult to undo in a hurry, often leaving a permanent kink where the knot was. The coated running lines have a slightly larger diameter, but tangle less and are no different than stripping a conventional full length line. My preference is the latter.

Manufactures sell all varieties of shooting heads, most with a built-in loop at both end of the lines. You can also manufacture your own from the Cortland LC 13 (13 grains per foot) lead core line. This was the staple of the steelhead fishermen when maximum sink was called for and is still popular as a head building material today. Rio has come out with a coated tungsten core line that is more supple than the LC 13 and comes in three sizes: 14 grain , 11 grain, and 8 grain per foot of line. Both types of lines come in thirty foot coils and one hundred foot spools.

Bottom Line

I personally like the versatility that shooting heads offer, from fast sinking to floating. They are an ideal choice if you want a full range of options, but have only one spool. They are not for everyone when it comes to casting, however, the advantage going to the integrated full length lines.

Backing

The main choice for backing is between Dacron or gel-spun lines. Dacron, until recently, was the backing of choice and I think a good case can be made for the selection of Dacron to this day. Dacron backing is strong for its diameter and lasts for several seasons. By comparison it is reasonable in price when you consider the hundreds of yards required to fill each reel spool. The gel-spun lines, often referred to as Spectra, have become quite popular in recent years. Gel-spun is extremely tough for its diameter and allows greater capacity on the spool. A typical gel-spun line in 50 pound test has the same diameter as 12 pound monofilament.

The up side to gel-spun is that you can run 50 pound test on the spool with greater capacity than 30 pound Dacron. The small diameter cuts through the water with very little drag, a plus when you consider the effect that water drag has on delicate leaders. Gel-spun is very tough when it comes to abrasion and affords excellent protection when your expensive fly line is somewhere hundreds of yards off the reel and streaking behind a striped Marlin train wreck.

Draw backs? There are some. Gel-spun is a lot more expensive than Dacron, especially if you have numerous reels and additional spools to fill. Gel-spun is very hard in texture and along with the small diameter can cut your fingers to the bone if you get a digit tangled with a fast running fish. The stuff is slippery when it comes to tying knots. Gel-spun can also cut deep into the wraps on a reel spool if care isn't taken to ensure that the line comes on the reel evenly and tightly. Is it worth it? To me the choice is an individual one and, among the partners in our guide business, we each have a different view. In our case, with some forty reels to fill and additional spools to accommodate different lines, right- or left-handed reeling set ups, expense is of a concern. Many, if not most of our clients are new to saltwater fly fishing and playing big fish on fly tackle. The concerns for angler safety and possible tangles deep in the backing have led us to using Dacron for most of our set ups. We do run Spectra on some of our billfish rigs and top shots of one hundred yards of Spectra on other heavy application reels.

For the recreational angler, Spectra makes good sense if you know how to offset the draw backs. The expense can be offset to an extent by buying in bulk. Spectra line lasts longer than Dacron, so the expense evens out over time. Line cuts can be avoided with awareness and fish fighting gloves or by taping your fingers with vet wrap. The slippery knot situation can be mitigated by choice of knots and by making more wraps or adding reverse twists when forming the connections. I use a Bimini twist to form the loop-to-loop connections from gel-spun to fly line and to join Dacron to a top shot of Spectra. The cinch knot part of the Bimini is where this connection can fail as the Spectra tends to slip out from under the wraps of the knot, especially when a uni knot is used. I put in an extra half hitch and use a ten turn nail knot to ensure the integrity of the union.

Gel-spun line is a definite plus if you have a conventional or mid-sized arbor, or a reel with smaller than desired capacity. If you're a steelhead or salmon fisherman making your first trip to the big salt, you might feel a bit queasy about laying out big bucks for a large capacity reel that may or may not see another trip. In most cases the rod size is appropriate for light to moderate duty, but the reel is on the small side of capacity. An alternative here, and one that I use, is to load a hundred yards of Spectra on top of the Dacron. The extra one hundred yards takes up very little capacity and provides the extra yardage.

What about using 20-pound Dacron backing on the smaller reels and go for more capacity? The 20-pound backing is certainly stronger than the 12- to 16-pound leader that we normally use on the 8 weight through 10 weight rigs. The drawback to 20-pound backing is that one little nick in the weave renders the line extremely weak and prone to breaking. The 30-pound line is much less apt to break if a small tear occurs in the fibers of the weave, at the very least allowing you time to recognize the problem and fix it before it costs you a fish.

Photograph by Brian O'Keefe

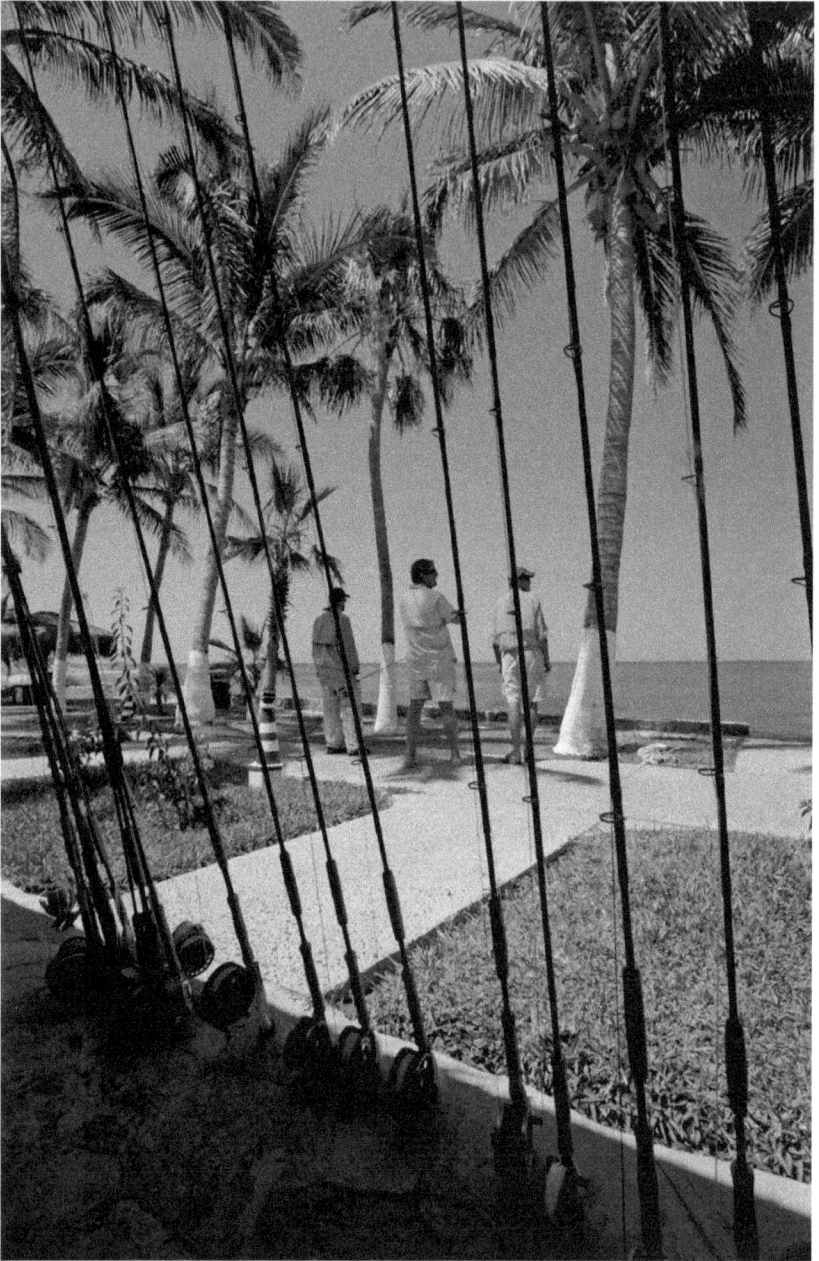

Photograph by Brian O'Keefe

3

Leaders and Knots:
Getting Connected

Leader systems and the knots that join the pieces are an absolutely critical component in saltwater fly fishing. The weakest point in our tackle choices come down to the leader and the knots that connect the parts. In this section I will look at the parts of the leader, the leader materials and finally I will break down the leaders into four categories including leaders for the beach, light inshore, blue water and billfish.

In our saltwater guiding, we keep our leaders selection and construction as simple as the situation allows and utilize a loop system to connect the various parts of the leader together. We also use loops to connect the leader to the fly line as well as connecting the fly line to the backing. My off shore guiding experience has lead me to the use of looped connections for the speed at which we can change whole leader systems, often with fly attached, to meet the ever changing conditions and species encountered. To further expedite the process, we keep a good supply of pre-tied leaders available for that quick change to match the new game in town, or to replace a frayed leader after landing a good fish. The loop-to-loop system carries over to the beach and inshore fishing situation as well. Factory-built tapered leaders work fine on the beach too, but do not offer the same advantages they lend in fresh water fishing

Leader Material

The qualities we look for in leader material include consistent breaking strength, abrasion resistance, knot strength, proper degree of stiffness, and in some cases, invisibility from the fish's perspective. In our situation as guides, being able to buy leader material in bulk is another consideration.

Consistent line strength is a must factor, though easily met by today's production standards. A caution should be noted here that unless the material is labeled IGFA rated, the actual breaking strength may be higher than stated on the label. This has implications for those interested in registering a line class record. The other factor is the leader can exceed the breaking strength of the rod or backing.

In saltwater fishing, abrasion resistance is very important given the small sharp teeth and gill covers found on many of the species encountered. A low back casts that drags through the sand will also eat up leader material (as well as flies and fly lines). Until recently that meant leader material was made thicker and stiffer to maintain strength while allowing for some abrasion. The stiff nature of the leader made knot tying tougher. Better life through chemistry has resulted in harder polymers, fluorocarbon and blends of materials. The modern leader material we prefer has supple inner cores for easier knot tying as well as a tough outer core for abrasion resistance. The newer blended, or co-polymer leaders have a high strength to diameter ratio that addresses both abrasion resistance and visibility issues. Fluorocarbon leader material has taken the fishing world by storm in some places. There are some distinct advantages to using fluorocarbon and some pitfalls that can be avoided.

The most common reason that anglers purchase fluorocarbon is for the refraction rate that makes the line less visible to the fish. To be honest I am not sure how important invisibility is to the species we pursuit on the Baja or elsewhere in the big salt, or if a smaller diameter leader accomplishes the same purpose. Tuna have shown a tendency to avoid flies tied to thicker leader material, especially when the presentation to the fish is on the dead drop. Part of this fickleness may be due to the affect that a thicker leader has on the action of the fly and the rate of sink.

Several falls ago we were fishing a yellowfin bite using live bait on 40 lb. mono. Other boats were hooking up while our clients were going fishless. I switched to a 20 lb. fluorocarbon leader and our folks immediately started picking up fish. Whether success was due to the change in diameter affecting the swimming of the live bait, or the visibility factor affected by fluorocarbon, I am not sure.

Applied to fly fishing, if fluorocarbon adds an invisibility advantage under tough conditions, why not use it? We have found one pitfall with fluorocarbon in that some of the knots we had been using tended to slip more than with nylon. This was especially true when connecting a class tippet to a heavy bite tippet due to the big difference in diameter and surface hardness of the two lines being joined.

My experience with fluorocarbon, when it first became available, was not a good one. The knots that I tied joining a fluorocarbon class leader to the one hundred pound bite tippet slipped at the Hufnagle knot on the first billfish. The client was disappointed to say the least. I was devastated for the client's sake and left with a quaking level of confidence in ever using fluorocarbon again. We have since learned how to mitigate this challenge by using different knots or improving the knots we were using by putting more twists into the construction of the knots. Knots such as the Yucatan, Eugene Bend or San Diego hold well in the particular fluorocarbon material I use. Loop-to-loop connections are unlikely to slip regardless of the material used. The important message here is to test your knots in the fluorocarbon leader you intend to use before you head south to fish.

There are other advantages to fluorocarbon leaders besides invisibility. The chemical properties of fluorocarbon are more impervious to the destructive effect of UV rays. Fluorocarbon absorbs less water and therefore retains greater knot strength when wet. The abrasion resistance of fluorocarbon is reputed to be greater than nylon. There is some speculation that the difference is due to the fluorocarbon lines having greater diameter for the same breaking strength than nylon. Another advantage is that fluorocarbon is denser than water and sinks faster than nylon. This can be a small advantage when fishing deep for tuna, pargo and pompano.

To address all of these factors in our business, we currently use the relatively new hybrid nylon and fluorocarbon blended lines, such as Yo-Zuri's original hybrid, and have been very satisfied with the results. P-line also makes a good product that blends nylon with fluorocarbon. The hybrid lines have a tough fluorocarbon outer layer that is less visible, resists abrasion and the effects of sun and water. The supple inner core is easy to form knots or join two lines of different diameter. In order to obtain leader material in sufficient quantity. we took a page from Lefty Kreh's book and used conventional reel filler spools of this high quality line for our class tippets. Modern methods of producing quality fishing line result in a high level of consistency comparable to the standards used in the manufacture of leader material. Again, a word of caution for those seeking IGFA records, Yo-Zuri and other quality lines on filler spools may have a higher breaking strength than stated on the label.

In saltwater fly fishing, there are two and sometimes three parts to the leader system. We will now look at these parts followed by the knots used to connect the parts, starting at the fly line and moving forward to the fly.

Butt Sections

All of our leader systems start with the butt section, the length and strength of which depends on the species we are after, and the type of fly line connected to the butt.

Not too many years ago, the common wisdom was to use a heavy, hard and stiff monofilament material for the butt section, such as Mason. We have found that a somewhat softer leader material facilitates a better transition from the soft forward section of fly line to the fly. The result is a better turn over transition of energy from the fly line to the leader along with easier material to work with and tie into knots.

The knots tied with the softer and smaller diameter material pass through the guides more easily. We highly discourage allowing the leader to be reeled into the rods guides, but it does happen with the excitement of landing a fish. Really bad things can happen when big knots go cracking through the rod guides at yellowfin speed.

The materials we favor for our butt sections include Jin Kai, Moi Moi and P-line. All have relatively small diameters to breaking strength, are abrasion resistant and tie easily. We generally match the size of the butt section leader material to the weight of the rod along these guidelines:

Eight to nine weight rods: 30 lb.
Ten to twelve weight rods: 40 lb.
Billfish: 50 lb.

Keep in mind that we are using a fairly soft and pliable material to build our butt sections. If limited to one spool of butt section, I would use 40 lb. for everything.

One of the newer innovations to our leader system is a ferruled butt section. This is a somewhat advanced approach to building butt sections with some advantages over the more basic single strand of line. The ferruled leader turns the fly over well while providing a great shock absorber that protects the knots and the more fragile class section of the leader. The top end of the leader is doubled over so that no knot forms the loop that connects to the loop in the fly line. This makes for a very smooth connection and mitigates the problem of the leader inadvertently sliding up into the guides of the rod. I tie my flies on Norm Norlander's rotary vice which is ideal for spinning the butt material into a ferruled leader. Ferruled leaders can also be produced with an electric drill. This is best done as a two-person operation.

To build a ferruled leader, I start with an arm span of leader material plus two feet. Tie a loop in one end and hang it on a hook attached to the drill or rotary vice. Come back to a full arm span length from the loop knot and make several wraps of the leader around your finger. This should leave two feet of leader hanging free. The idea here is to prevent the last two feet of material from twisting.

Spin the vice or start your drill, twisting the leader between the vice/drill and where the line is wrapped around your finger. When the line is adequately twisted, you will feel the leader shorten in your hand. Take the loop end off of the hook attached to the vice/drill. Find the midpoint in the twisted section of leader and place the midpoint on the hook in the vice, thus doubling the line back on itself so that the two lengths are parallel to each other and equal in length in the twisted portion. The untwisted portion will still extend beyond the point you are holding it with your fingers.

Remember to keep hold of the last two feet of untwisted leader during this process so it doesn't gain a twist. Place and hold the end of the twisted line with the hook loop together with the still untwisted section. Be careful not to let the two sections of line twist together on their own until reattached to the vice. Believe me, left on their own, they will twist together and you will end up with a kinked, knotted up mess.

Once the middle point of the twisted portion of the leader is attached to the hook on the vice or drill, let the vice rotate in the opposite direction that the original twist was formed, allowing the two strands to twist together in a controlled manner.

Once the two strands have twisted together, take the leader off of the vice and secure the open end of the twisted strands together (next to where the free strand is wrapped around your finger) with a double overhand knot. Your butt section now has about two and a half feet of twisted double strand and two feet of untwisted single strand, so in essence a tapered butt section.

Complete the butt section with a perfection loop in the single strand. The top end of the butt section will have a loop created when you doubled the line back on itself. Connect this to a loop on the fly line. Since the loop was formed by folding the line without a knot, there is nothing to hang in the top guide of the fly rod if you inadvertently reel the leader into the rod guide.

Butt Section Knots

For a single-strand butt section, the simplest knot system starts with perfection loops tied to each end of the butt section. We tie a one inch loop into the fly line end of the butt section and a two inches loop on the class tippet side.

The larger loop expedites changing class tippet, bite tippet and big fly all in one easy motion. The perfection loop, while not the strongest knot you can choose, is definitely stronger than the breaking strength of the class tippet. The perfection knot is fast to tie, and is less bulky than the double surgeons or king sling.

In a ferruled leader system, the top loop is formed after the line is twisted and doubled back on itself. The leader end in the single strand section is also finished with a perfection loop of two inches.

Perfection Loop

This is a compact knot that forms a small loop in the end of a leader or to connect a swivel or hook with when the intent is to let the hook swing. I used to doubt the strength of this knot until I watched many local Mexican Captains successfully use this knot to attach a hook for yellowfin tuna in 40 lb. mono.

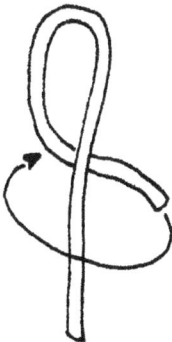

STEP 1: Make a loop at the end of the line by passing the tag end behind the standing line.

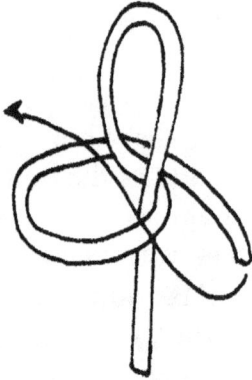

STEP 2: Make a turn around the standing line forming a loop. Hold that in place and make another turn around the line, crossing on the top side of the new loop.

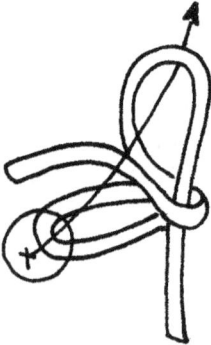

STEP 3: Hold the tag end in place and pass the second loop through the first loop.

STEP 4: Pull the second loop up until a knot forms tight. Trim the tag end.

Class Tippet

The class tippet is the second part of a saltwater leader, and in many cases the last part, connecting directly to the fly. This is the weakest part of the line leader system and deserves careful consideration of both knots and the leader material used.

We size the breaking strength of the class leader according to the weight of the rod. In the world of saltwater fly fishing, rods do break. Oversizing the breaking strength of the leader relative to the weight of the rod definitely ups the odds of turning a nice four piece rod into an ugly five or six piecer. Also bear in mind that each rod weight rapidly reaches a point of diminishing return in its ability to lift or pull a fish. Exceed that point and something has to give, hopefully it's a ten cent leader and not an expensive rod.

The general rule of thumb I use in matching class tippet to rod weight is as follows:

> 8 weight and 9 weight rods = 6 to 12 lb. test leader (3 to 5 kilo).

> 10 weight and 11 weight rods = 12 to 16 lb. test leader (6 to 8 kilo).

> 12 weight rods and above = 20 lb. test leader (10 kilo).

This is the general rule of thumb that we use in our business for most all of our leaders whether we are fishing from the shore or chasing blue water species.

Knots for the Class Tippet

Several knots work well in the class tippet in order to make a loop-to-loop connection to the butt section. To form a single small loop in the class tippet, I have had very good luck with either a king sling (also known as the end loop), or double surgeon's knot.

The use of a single loop connection is generally limited to the pursuit of smaller shoreline species, or when speed in tying up a leader is of the utmost importance. I use far more double loop connections, especially with big fish in mind.

The double loop is formed from a single large loop doubled back and tied together with a surgeon's knot or king sling. The double loops spread the pressure over more surface area at the connection point with the butt section, making it a much stronger union.

To form the initial large single loop, I use the king sling, spider hitch or the Bimini twist. The later knot, though more challenging to learn, has proven to be the strongest knot when using light tippets on large fish. The twist in the Bimini knot has a springy action that absorbs the jerks created by head shakes from powerful fish. The Bimini is my choice for billfish, and other big offshore species.

The spider hitch or king sling are both strong knots in their own right and are faster and easier to tie than the Bimini. The king sling is a better choice if your intent is to form a small loop, such as an anchor for the Yucatan or bristle knot. It is excellent for forming the small single loop that attaches to the butt section. If you struggle with the Bimini, the king sling or spider hitches have very nearly the same breaking strength, while easier and faster for most people to tie. I am of the mind that the knot you tie best, is going to be your strongest knot. Keep in mind that if you use a ferruled butt section the shock absorption factor increases the viability of any knot.

King Sling or End Loop Knot

This is an easy-to-tie loop knot that I use to connect leader sections together, or as the base to tie a Yucatan knot. It tests very strong on the Knot Machine.

STEP 1: Form an open loop of line approximately 6 inches long.

STEP 2: Double the loop you just formed back over and parallel to itself.

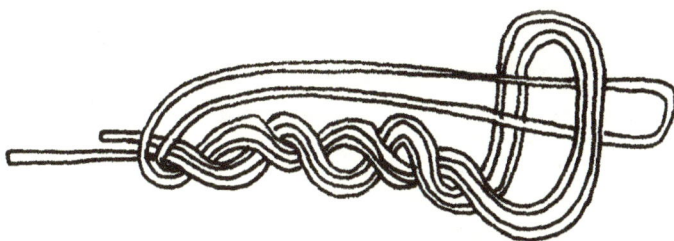

STEP 3: Holding the original loop and standing line in the left hand, twist the second formed loop with the right hand three times.

STEP 4: Pass the first formed loop back through the second formed loop.

STEP 5: To tighten, moisten and hold the loop and pull the standing line and tag end at the same time. Trim the tag end.

Eugene Bend

This simple and quick knot is the one I use most often to attach the fly to the class leader. I tested this on the Berkley Trilene Knot Machine against the San Diego knot and the Uni Knot and it won hands down.

STEP 1: Pass the line through the eye of the hook or fly. Double back over the main line.

STEP 2: With the doubled line, make 3 turns over the standing line.

STEP 3: Thread the formed end loop of the doubled line over the open end of the starter line.

STEP 4: Make sure the knot lies even and parallel, moisten with saliva and cinch tight. When tied properly, the tag end of the knot will pop forward with a noticeable click. If it doesn't pop forward cut it off and retie.

Spider Hitch

The Spider Hitch is an excellent knot for quickly forming a double line when light tackle fishing.

STEP 1: Double over the line and form a loop.

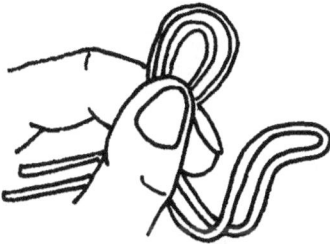

STEP 2: Hold the loop between thumb and forefinger.

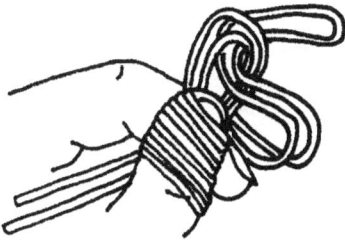

STEP 3: Wrap the doubled line around the thumb and the loop five times. Then pass the end of the double line through the loop. Slowly pull on the double line allowing the loops to unwind off the thumb.

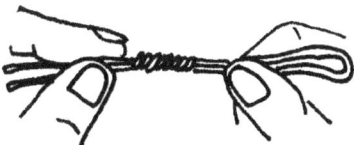

STEP 4: Moisten with saliva and pull evenly on all four ends to tighten.

Bimini Twist

This knot is considered by many the most reliable way to make a double line at either end of a class leader and to connect to the butt section, the fly or the bite leader.

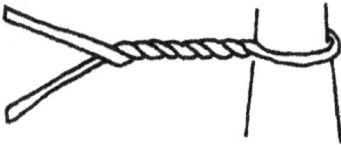

STEP 1: Double the line into a loop and make 16 to 20 twists in the end of the loop. Slip the open end over your knee and keep constant pressure on both ends of the loop. Spread your hands apart, forcing the twists downward towards your knee. For a longer doubled line, run the loop down to your feet and over your knees.

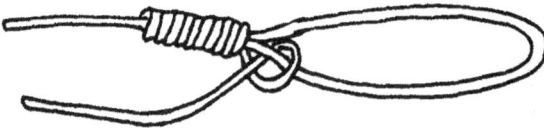

STEP 2: Lower the hand holding the tag end until it slips back over the first twists. Open the angle of the loop with a finger (or spread your knees apart if the loop is over both knees) and let tag end roll over the column of twists. Keep the tag end at a right angle and roll to the end of the twists.

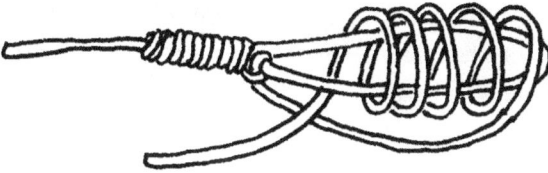

STEP 3: After the end is rolled down to the end of the twists, make a half-hitch on the near side of the loop to lock everything in place. Be sure to maintain tension on all lines.

STEP 4: Release knee pressure, but keep the loop tight, and secure the knot by making 4 to 6 reverse wraps as in a Uni knot around both lines of the loop. Carefully pull the tag end so that all of the reverse wraps are closed tight against the base of the half hitch holding the Bimini in place.

I do a variation on the standard Bimini that I find holds more reliably. The difference begins after the half hitch is in place holding the Bimini together. I secure the Bimini with a nail knot instead of the reverse wraps and begin by placing a loop of wire or mono parallel to the leader above the half hitch, with the loop in the wire/mono pointing away from the hitch.

I wrap the tag end of line forward over the loop and leader, pass the tag end through the loop in the wire/mono and pull the tag back under the wraps.

Yucatan or Bristol Knot

Is an easy and excellent knot to join a heavy bite leader to the class leader. It is also useful to attach spectra to mono. The Yucatan Knot is also known as the Bristol Knot.

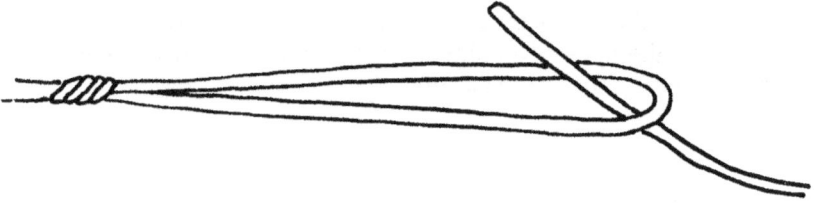

STEP 1: Make a short loop in the class leader using a Bimini Twist, King Sling or a Spider Hitch. Pass the heavy bite leader through the loop. A variation on this knot is to form an open loop (no knot forming the loop) in the class leader.

Once the knot on the heavy leader side is pulled tight a nail knot or Uni knot can be used to form and hold the loop in place up against the Yucatan in the heavy bite leader. I use this for IGFA leader systems to shorten up the knot on the bite leader.

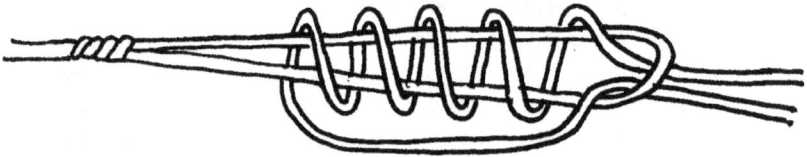

STEP 2: Wrap the bite leader around the loop in the leader five times.

STEP 3: Bend the tag end of the bite leader back on itself and pass it through the end of the loop passing through the loop the same side it went in. Lubricate with saliva and carefully pull tight. The two lines will wrap around each other. Trim the tag end of the leader close.

STEP 4: The finished knot is compact and strong when attaching a class leader to a heavy bite leader, and it casts well and passes through rod guides easily when used to attach a top shot of mono to spectra.

Bite Tippet

The bite tippet, (also known as the shock tippet or bite leader), when used, is the connection between the class tippet and the fly. The bite tippet serves several purposes. The first and most obvious is to protect the class tippet from the teeth or bills of certain species that we commonly encounter. The toothy species include the sierra mackerel and wahoo. For these speedsters, the use of wire as a bite tippet is preferred, twenty pound for the former and sixty pound test for the later. The bill on a sailfish or marlin plays havoc with class leaders, necessitating the addition of a bite tippet of 80- to 100-pound test monofilament or fluorocarbon.

Most species found on the Baja do not require the use of a bite tippet, but there are times when I still add one to the leader system. In the case of dorado destined to be released, I add a bite tippet of 40- to 50-pound test. Dorado can be difficult to land by hand without grabbing and breaking the delicate class tippet. The addition of a bite tippet gives you a more durable handle to control the fish's head at boat side. Once the head is under control by one hand, your other hand can grab the tail or lip with a Boga grip to hoist the fish aboard.

Bite tippets are often used on trolling setups intended for dorado and tuna with the possibility of tangling with other species. A good number of sailfish and marlin have come to the boat on such rigs due to the addition of a heavy bite tippet.

As is the case with the butt section, I have moved away from the stiff, high diameter leader material, in favor of the softer co-polymers. My preference for bite tippet material is the same for the butt section. I have had great success with the products made by Moi Moi or Jin Kai. Knots are easier to tie in a softer monofilament, hold better and have a smaller profile. Fluorocarbon has become so popular as a bite leader with conventional fishermen that it is getting hard to find a good source of soft nylon. Personally, I feel that fluorocarbon is an overkill for this application if abrasion is your concern. We have landed lots of billfish on 80- and 100-pound nylon leader without losing one to abrasion. The class leader is the weak spot in a fly fishing leader system and the point that most break-offs occur.

Bite Tippet to Class Tippet Knots

As stated earlier, the class tippet is the critical link in the leader system. The weakest point in the system is where the class tippet is joined to the bite tippet. This is in large part due to the difference in diameter between the parts being joined, as well as the difference in stiffness and surface texture of the leader material.

Knots such as the Hufnagle and Albright have been used for years and are very good knots when properly tied. The Hufnagle is a difficult knot for some anglers to tie correctly and is bulky when finished. The Albright is easier to tie, but lays the bite tippet somewhat askew of the straight line in the class tippet. The knot I have come to rely on in recent years is the Yucatan or Bristol knot.

For most people, this is the easiest knot of all to tie. It is a small compact knot that lies straight in line with the class leader. The Yucatan knot can be attached to a loop for non-IGFA situations, or directly to the class leader with a nail knot or uni-knot cinch, similar in approach to the slim beauty. I prefer the direct connection as it eliminates the second loop knot in the class leader and results in a very small connection to the bite tippet. This leader set up is gaining popularity here on the Baja as well with the tarpon fisher-men in the Florida Keys. Here again, I recommend that you use the knot that you tie best and most consistently.

Terminal Knots

Not to be confused with knots to die for, the last knot we are concerned with is the one tied directly to the fly. Knot selection is vast and somewhat confusing as the names of knots vary with location and who is credited with the creation of the knot. I will try to sort through some of this as we discuss the various knots. With so many options, I will restate here that the choice should come down to the knots you tie best.

To get started. let's break down the situations and the knots that best apply.

Much of our choice depends on if the fly is connected to the class tippet or the bite tippet. The other broad choice is whether we want the fly to swing freely at the end of the leader, or whether we want a solid connection.

Let's look at the most critical connection, the connection to the class tippet first. We have no margin for error here, so the knot must be as close to the breaking strength of the leader as we can tie. Looped and solid connections will get us close. So, which do we use?

There is a fairly even split between guides and experienced saltwater writers about the selection with eminent advocates for either approach. I'll give you my thoughts on this subject and you can take it from there. The main thing is that you must tie a good knot every time. I tend to tie a solid connection when I am using a fly that is stripped fast from the time it hits the water, or with flies that may turn on their side with a fast retrieve. My favorite knots are the Eugene Bend and the San Diego knot, also known as the tuna knot. Other serviceable knots include improvements to the clinch knot when the standing line is either doubled through the eye of the hook, or when a reverse twist is added towards the opening in the line at the eye of the hook. The Palomar knot is another good choice.

I like using a loop knot when I fish a fly on the dead drop to tuna, jacks, pargo and others. In these situations my fly of choice is usually a Clouser-style tie. The loop connection allows the Clouser to hop and swoop more freely. The loop connection also seems to give better action to flies that swing or wobble due to the construction in the head. In other words, flies that have large round heads such as the Mosca Magic, barbell eyes such as the Clouser, or cupped faces such as a crease fly work better when they can swing. This is especially true when we connect the fly to the heavy bite tippet. My favorite connection is Lefty's Loop knot. Lefty has disavowed credit for creating the knot, but the name remains connected to him. I have seen this knot also referred to as the loop knot and the 100% knot.

When connecting to a heavy bite tippet, I make the choice of loop versus solid knot for the same reason as I do when connecting to the class tippet. I do use different knots though. For a solid connection the Eugene Bend gives way to a clinch knot with a three-turn, reverse twist back to the gap at the eye of the hook. The loop knot that I use most, is the Lefty loop knot, but again with just three twists.

San Diego Knot

This knot is also called a Reverse Cinch, Tuna or Helliger knot, and is popular on long-range fishing charters.

STEP 1: Pass the line through the eye of the hook or fly. Double back over the main line.

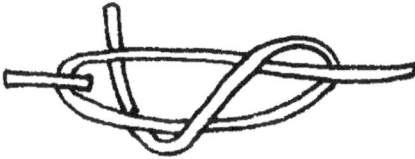

STEP 2: Begin making turns over the main line. The number of turns varies with the line size, from 8 turns with 10 lb. line down to 3 turns with 40 lb.

STEP 3: Complete the appropriate number of turns, then thread the tag end of the first loop above the eye.

STEP 4: Holding the coils in place, pass the tag end through the loop created by the last coil of the knot.

STEP 5: Hold the tag end and standing line while pulling up the coils. Make sure the coils are in a spiral, not overlapping each other. Slide against the eye. Clip the tag end.

Lefty's Loop or Non-Slip Loop Knot

This loop knot does not slip and will break at near 100% of the line strength rating.

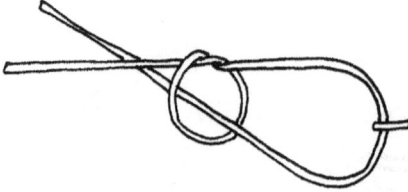

STEP 1: Make an overhand knot in the line about 10 inches from the end. Pass the tag end through the eye and back through the loop of the overhand knot.

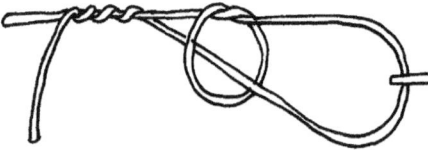

STEP 2: Wrap the tag end around the standing line about 5 times. Bring the tag end back through the overhand knot, entering from the same side it exited from before.

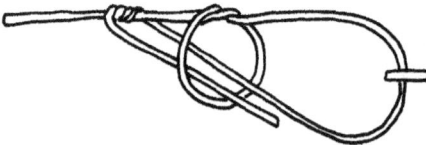

STEP 3: Moisten the knot and then pull slowly on the tag end to tighten the wraps loosely together.

STEP 4: Pull the loop and the standing line in opposite directions to set the knot. Trim the tag end.

Leaders

Leaders for the Beach

As previously stated, I do not use factory tapered leaders as a matter of personal preference and economy. A formula for a simple leader that turns over well, is built with a butt section four feet long of 30 or 40 lb. soft mono, connected to three or more feet of class tippet via loop to loop. Tie a perfection loop in both the leader-to-fly-line connection and the leader-to-class tippet connection. In most shore fishing situations, a bite tippet is not necessary and may even reduce the number of hook ups. The notable exception here is when the sierra are marauding the beaches at first light with their razor sharp teeth. In this situation a bite tippet of #2 wire or 15 lb. braided wire is in order.

Ferruled leaders are generally comprised of three and a half to four feet of butt section. Two feet of which is twisted double strand that transitions down to two feet of single strand ending with a perfection loop. Three to four feet of class tippet is connected by loops to the butt section. Leaders can be lengthened or shortened pending water clarity, spooky fish, and wind.

Leaders for In-Shore

The leader systems that I prefer for species found in the green water world are essentially a shorter version of my beach leaders. A three foot butt section of ferruled or single-strand, soft mono followed by three feet of class tippet has served me well for roosters from the boat, skipjack, bonito, pargo, ladyfish, jack crevalle and a host of others. The leaders are shorter by design to facilitate the handling of fish at boat side. Long leaders, long rods and short deck space makes for awkward landings. As in most beach situations a bite leader is not necessary unless sierras are lurking.

Leaders for the Blue Water

The blue water world is demanding of all tackle components and especially the leader system. It is also a world in which any manner of finned species may show up for lunch. My first hook up on a sailfish came while throwing small flies into a feeding frenzy of dorado. Notice that I say hook up, as without a bite leader the fight lasted until the first spiraling pirouette wrapped the sixteen pound leader around an abrasive bill and the fish was gone.

Is there a leader for all blue water situations? In my experience there are more situations than what a single-minded approach will cover. Some principles do apply to most situations that include keeping the whole leader as short as the situation allows. Starting with the butt section, I suggest two to three feet of ferruled or soft, single strand in 40 lb. test. I prefer a two foot butt section if I am adding a bite leader to the system, so that the overall leader is six feet or less.

The class tippet should match the rod strength and be kept fairly short. I tie mine on average between 18 to 24 inches. The bite leader is where the variations occur. On trolling rigs, I use 50 lb. to 100 lb. bite pending the odd strike from a billfish. They do like the Mosca Magic, a fly we troll often, to locate dorado and tuna. When wahoo are around, the bite leader is 60 lb. wire.

If you are fishing IGFA, the bite leader cannot exceed twelve inches including the knots. If records are not a concern, I like a bite of 24 to 30 inches. The longer bite leader facilitates the handling of the fish at boat side, especially if the intent is to release the fish.

Once a school has been located and we are casting to fish, I switch to a rod with a leader built with casting and stripping in mind. If the target is dorado or tuna, the bite leader is left off and the fly is attached directly to the class leader. Small to medium sized fish of both species have small teeth, but seldom pose a problem of abrasion to warrant a bite leader. When the dorado run bigger, say thirty pounds or larger, I do attach a 40 lb. bite to the class leader for extra protection against their teeth.

Leaders for Billfish

Billfish leaders serve the specific purpose of handling some of the most explosive fighting capability you can experience. I build my leaders as short as possible to facilitate handling the fish at boat side. I like a ferruled butt section of 18 inches of 50 lb. looped to 16 inches of 10 kg class leader. To this I add a bite leader of 80 or 100 lb. test. If fishing IGFA, the length of the bite is kept to 12 inches including the knots. Otherwise my bite leaders are 30 to 36 inches long. The longer bite leader is safer for the deck hand to handle, without coming in contact with the bill, if the fish should try to jump while attempting to grab the leader.

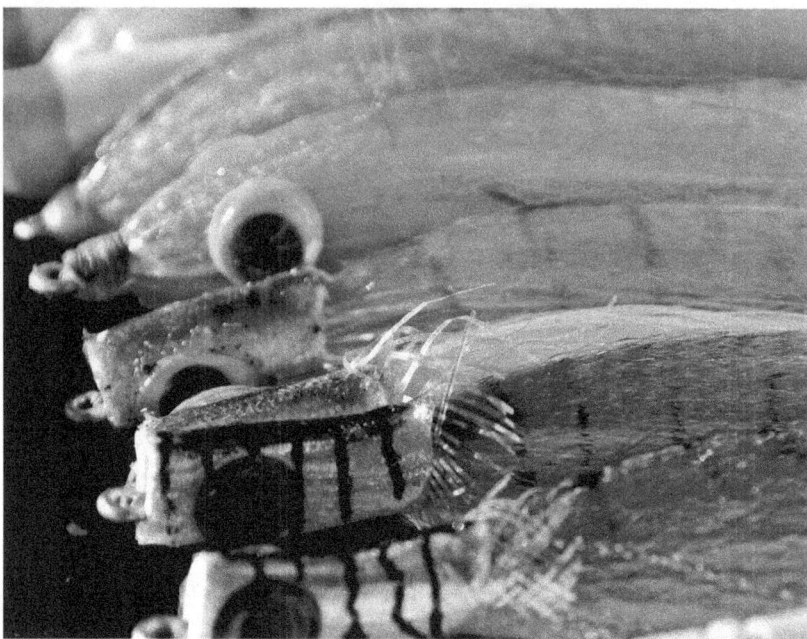

Photograph by Eric Kummerfeldt

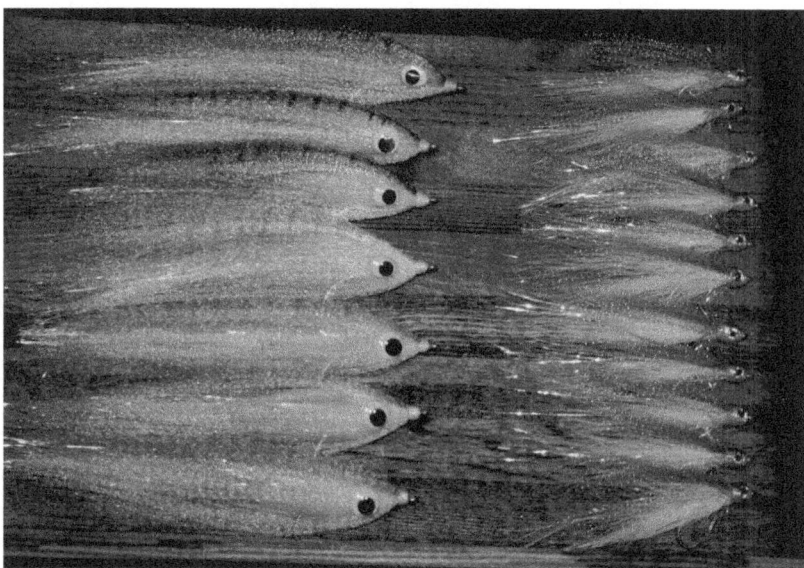

Photograph by the author

4

Flies for all Occasions: A Saltwater Match the Hatch

We do a lot of sport shows and fishing club presentations in trout country where we display the flies that we use while fishing the salt. Quite commonly the first reaction from folks is something along the lines of, "Jeeze look at the size of that fly. Saltwater fly fishing is sure different than trout fishing".

Being a contemplative sort, I have given a lot of thought to the differences and similarities of trout fishing and saltwater, big-game fishing and more importantly how to relate the two experiences. I have come to the conclusion that the principles are much the same when it comes to fly selection.

In trout fishing, we often fish attractor patterns when no hatch is present, or we match the hatch when bugs or feeding activity is present especially to selective fish. In saltwater, the situation is very much the same in the use of large, often flashy flies to locate fish when there is no feeding activity apparent. Once fish are found working bait fish or chum, the game changes. Most saltwater species are very much like trout in that, when a predominate food source is present, the fish become selective to that food source and ignore other items on the menu.

This hit home for me many years ago while fishing for perch in San Francisco Bay. I was using pile worms and catching a fish now and then when a commercial fisherman tied his Whaler up to a piling in front of me and started to chum the water with grass shrimp. The fisherman apologized to me and warned me that once he put a lot grass shrimp in the water the perch would not want anything else. Sure enough, in about two minutes he began to haul in one perch after another using the same grass shrimp for bait. The modest action that I had enjoyed prior to his arrival evaporated with the bay fog and I silently cursed his family lineage. We eventually became friends and fished together often. In the process, I learned a lot about fish feeding behavior and ways to take advantage of their habits.

I have witnessed this same feeding behavior many times since, and have applied that experience to fly fishing saltwater species. The principles are much the same as for trout, once a hatch or movement of insects occurs.

Thirty years ago, my favorite fly was Joe Brook's blond pattern, comprised of a simple white tail and high style bucktail wing with silver tinsel wrapped around the hook shank. I love to tinker with the flies that I tie, so I go armed with boxes and boxes of the latest new flies. Despite my penchant to experiment, I have no doubt the simple blond pattern would still catch fish today with its predominately white body, good profile and movement. The deceiver and Clouser designs were very important additions to the saltwater fly fishing world along with the many variations that followed. Thirty years of observation, new tying materials available and lots of experimentation has led to some improvements on the blond, deceiver and Clouser, but the principle of the originals still work and form the base for new fly development.

In matching the saltwater hatch, the first key to fly selection is duplicating the size of the fly to the natural food being eaten. The live chum in the bait tank is a good place to start when selecting the size of fly you tie on. The shape of the fly is likewise very important. Many of the species we pursue, such as the tuna, often attack from below, so the silhouette, as viewed from the fish's perspective, should taper much like a torpedo from a broad head to a narrow tail. Flies used for species that attack from the side (e.g. the dorado) or rear (e.g. roosterfish) should match the tail and side profiles.

The next important feature I consider is movement. The material used to tie the fly should flow and move in the water, yet not collapse into a pencil shape at a fast retrieve. Bucktail and other natural fibers remain an important part of the construction of the flies I tie. I also employ flash material such as flashabou, for the sake of movement and crystal flash for a mirror-like reflection of mixed color.

Over the years, I have found that highly effective flies have large heads that push water and thereby gain response from the fish's lateral line. Large epoxy heads on the Mosca Magic, bar bell eyes on the Clouser, clipped deer hair on our mullet pattern, and the Gym Sock pattern all push water and catch fish.

Trigger mechanisms are critical to convincing a finicky feeder that the fly is alive and edible, and I incorporate the concept into the flies I tie. The "come eat me triggers" include flash, movement, eyes, or color contrasts.

Color of the fly also plays a role, though I think to a lesser degree than some of the other features. Most of the common bait fish, and especially sardinas, are largely a pearlescent white on the bottom and sides with a small dark dorsal. If the fish attacks from the bottom, the top color doesn't figure in at all.

My diving experience around bait balls has given me some useful insight to fly design, especially as it applies to color. I have spent hours following pods of sardinas noting several aspects that stand out. One of the first is that the dark dorsal color contrast that you see on the sardina in the bait tank quickly fades to light grey under about three feet of water. The overall color of the sardinas is pearlescent white to grey with a discernable dark blue lateral line radiated with gold highlights. As the school turns in unison, the sun reflects off individual fish with flashes of pearl surrounded by an aura of rainbow hues. Shades of pink, green, blue and chartreuse flash and fade with each turn of school. With these observations in mind, I often incorporate rainbow or mixed color crystal flash into the wings of my patterns. I often mix different colors of hair to achieve the rainbow effect.

The second feature that stands out is the black crescent on the tails of bait fish. The theory is that the bait fish follow the tail in front of them as an indication of how the rest of the school will turn, so as to remain in a tight, protective ball. I think that predators key in on this tail feature as well, so out comes the permanent marker to paint the tail of the fly black.

Common Bait Species

There are a number of species of bait found in the tropical Pacific, and recognizing which food the fish prefer is important. In the Sea of Cortez that means tying on an imitation of the flatiron herring or sardina as they are called by the local Mexican Captains.

This small baitfish is usually two to four inches in length with a pearlescent white belly and a darker dorsal that varies in color. We find sardinas with olive, tan, grey, black or blue backs. My sardina imitations incorporate a lot of pearlescent flash, especially when the intended fish is dorado, skipjack or tuna. Less flash in the tie is more effective on roosters.

The bulk of the flies we use in our guide business are either white or pearl with a narrow contrasting top. Over the years we have caught a lot of species on olive over white Clouser minnows tied on 1/0 to 3/0 hooks. A good variation to this is the half-and-half tied with a white deceiver tail and an olive/white Clouser wing. I particularly like the Clouser design of flies for several reasons. The Clouser, when properly tied, can be retrieved at high rate of speed while remaining stable in the water. In other words it doesn't tend to roll on its side with a hard hand strip or sweep of the fly line. This is a sure way to lose the interest of about any game fish following the fly.

Another innovation with the Clouser design, is to tie the pattern on a 60 degree bend jig hook. The advantage of this hook design is the strong keel effect to the swimming action of the fly. The pattern can be tied with a fuller under wing without turning the fly sideways when stripped fast.

Fish use their lateral line to detect the movement of bait fish and the large head on the Clouser seems to send out some good vibrations. The heavy weight at the head provides stability at a steady fast retrieve or a swooping and darting action when jigged. The weighted head is ideal for times when the fly is fished on the dead drop. Another reason to use lots of Clousers is that they are easy to tie in large quantities and are highly adaptive to a variety of materials.

One of the most effective and recently developed roosterfish flies that we use in our guide service is called the Baja bucktail deceiver or BBD. The fly is a combination of features found in the bucktail deceiver and the sea habit. It flows well in the water with its flared, multiple bucktail collars and further pushes water with a large epoxy head. The BBD's design characteristics provide good stability when ripped in front of pursuing roosterfish.

The rasta has claimed a number of good roosters, jacks and dorado for us. The dressing is reminiscent of the bucktail deceiver in that the tail is preceded by a series of collars. In this case the collar material is fox hair. The fly has good movement in the water, a bulky head that pushes water, and is stable when ripped through the water. I use them for both sardina and mullet imitations and select the size based on the length of the natural bait.

Other effective sardina imitations, include variations of the sardina, able sardina, sea habits, Lefty's deceivers, salmar-macs, whistlers and various poppers and crease flies. All of these patterns work well in olive/white, tan/white, chartreuse/white or blue/white, tied on 1/0 to 3/0 hooks.

The Mosca Magic is a signature fly developed by my partner John Matson and was originally intended as a sardina imitation for fishing dorado. The fly is made up almost entirely of pearl flashabou and crystal flash and finished with a large round epoxy head.

We have caught everything in the Sea of Cortez on this pattern, including sailfish, wahoo and striped marlin. It is especially deadly on dorado, skipjack and yellowfin tuna. When John and I joined up our two guide businesses, he proudly showed me his Mosca pattern and I have to admit I was a little skeptical of that much flash in an every-day-go-to pattern. I was going through a subtle is better stage at the time. After years of observing the reaction of fish to the fly, the Mosca has proven to be so effective that we have incorporated more flash into many of the flies we tie, including the extension of a flash tail on most patterns.

Further south and into Central America the flat iron herring becomes less common. Here its larger cousin, the thread fin herring is an important baitfish. They are similar in coloration and general body shape to the flat iron herring, but much larger in size. The local captains also refer to them as sardinas. Baja bucktail deceivers and rastas tied four to six inches make good imitations.

Ballyhoo and needlefish make up a large part of both in shore and off shore species diet. During April, May and June, small ballyhoo are thick along the beaches of the East Cape where the jacks and roosterfish can be found feeding on them.

The small ballyhoos are four to six inches long with light green to blue backs. To imitate the hatch, our number one fly is a long skinny Clouser-style fly we call the clouserhoo. The eyes are tied above the hook point and a thread beak is tied forward to the hook eye as in the tarpon style. The body is a sparse mix of white super hair belly and light blue or green topping. The lateral line is pearl or electric blue flashabou and halo comprised of a few strands of pearl crystal flash complete the fly.

Mullet are an important food source for big roosters and jacks. They are found from Southern California to South America. Mullet range in size from four inch cigars to twelve inches in length and longer. Their coloration match-es the sandy bottoms of the beaches where they feed on plankton and algae. Cream sides and tan to light olive tops cover the color spectrum. A dark tail crescent and big eyes are predominate characteristics of the mullet and one or both should be incorporated into the fly's design. The two patterns that we fish most are the Gym Sock and the Baja Muddler on 4/0 to 6/0 hooks and lengths to 10 inches. Other popular patterns are the rasta and beach rat.

Squid also make up a good part of the diet of all blue wa-ter species and a few squid patterns in the box can save the day. The squid pattern that we tie has a long body via a tube extension on a 5/0 to 8/0 hook. The bigger squid patterns can be deadly on striped marlin. Humboldt squid can change color in an instant, but often show red to pink spots on a white to tan colored body. We dress our flies accordingly.

When natural bait is absent, we often try large attractor patterns in red/white, yellow/red purple/black, chartreuse/ white and yellow/green. Large deceiver or Clouser-style flies also work well. These same flies can be used to troll with to locate schools of fish. Large flies and poppers work best early and late in the day, while smaller and sparsely dressed flies seem to be more effective during the middle of the day.

Without a doubt, the flies used in any fly fishing situa-tion are a key element to your success. They can fascinate and charm us to buy, tie and horde way more than we will ever fish. Reminiscing back on the action of the day inspires new pattern designs, especially if the fish were persnickety. I know fly fishermen that fish as an excuse to create new flies and at times find myself focused on the tying bench when I could be on the beach fishing. Fly fishermen who don't tie can be almost as obsessive about having enough of the right fly in the hottest new pattern. After all, it wouldn't be fly fishing without the fly, or the fly gear we discussed in previous chapters.

So, is there a silver bullet fly, one that works better than all the rest? It's possible and the quest to develop it is part of the attraction to fly fishing.

In the mean time, here are the characteristics that I find effective in the patterns that I use.

One, they should be sized and shaped to approximate the size of the baitfish, keeping mind that the profile of the fly could be viewed from below as well as from the side and from the rear.

Two, the fly should have movement built into the wing, tail and body.

Three, the fly needs to be proportioned to ride true in the water, no twisting or turning when ripped.

Four, consider sonic line impression.

Five, include trigger mechanisms such as flash tails, black tail tips or eyes.

Six, include a variety of colors with your patterns.

With all this being said, the fly is important, but is only one piece of the puzzle. To me, how we present the fly and the why behind it, is yet the bigger piece. That is what the following chapters are about.

Photograph by Brian O'Keefe

Photograph by Brian O'Keefe

5

Getting Hooked Up:
Presentation, Presentation, Presentation, or How to be a Better Stripper

Fishing was once described to me as an activity where the most intelligent life form on earth tries to out think a critter with a brain the size of a pea. I know fly fishermen who approach the sport with no less mental preparation than an international chess match. Over kill? Perhaps it is, but for many of us it is a good part of the fun. Being a fishing guide gives me the opportunity to hear scads of theories and answers to the great mysteries surrounding convincing a small-brained creature to eat hair, feathers and fiber served on a hook. Along the way, I too, get to dabble in the chess game and ponder the great mysteries.

My purpose in this chapter is to discuss some broad tactical approaches to getting a fish to actually eat the fly. Along the way I will contrast the tactics that catch fish, compared to those that merely elicit a follow. I will also discuss aspects of the mental game in applying fish feeding behavior to how to present the fly. I have made many references in this book to the similarities of approach in saltwater fly fishing to trout and other fresh water species, especially in the context of fish feeding behavior. That theme will run strong in this chapter.

My thoughts on this subject come from thirty years of pursuing saltwater species and in particular roosterfish and the thousands of refusals that I have witnessed as a guide and experienced as an angler. What we collectively have learned on, the rooterfish, one of the toughest fish to fool, can be applied to the other species pursued in the saltwater; therefore I will focus much of this chapter on this challenging specie.

For many years, the success I experienced on roosters seemed somewhat random, especially in the early years when catches of the larger fish were far too infrequent. This began to change as I came to the realization that there is a pattern of feeding behavior that signals whether the fish will actually eat the fly or merely follow and refuse. I was excited every time a rooster would follow my fly to the rod tip, even though in the end they invariably refused my offering. I worked hard at trying variations on old themes that worked well in getting the fish to follow. My reasoning at the time was, that if the fish would follow the fly, surely they would eat the fly and that success would come if I changed flies, created a better fly or tried the same fly in a different color.

If a fast retrieve didn't work, I would slow the pace down. This thought pattern of presentation didn't change much until it hit me that the act of eating and the act of following are in many instances two entirely different behaviors, one originating in curiosity the other a desire to fill its belly. Roosterfish, in my experience, tend to respond to bait, fly and lure out of curiosity more often than other species.

By contrast their cousin the jack crevalle is either going to eat our offering or ignore it. This can leave the impression that the jack is easier to catch because they don't refuse the fly at the last instant as the result of a curious follow. This is not to say that the curious roosterfish won't become a feeding roosterfish. In some instances, and with the right approach, this does occur.

For me, the key to greater success came with greater understanding of feeding behavior. When I began to focus on what gets them to eat rather than repeating the approach that only results in a follow, more hook ups were the result. Along the way I have come to accept the brutal truth that not all fish, and especially roosterfish, are catchable, even if they give a good follow to the fly.

This leads to the second part of understanding roosterfish behavior in terms of differentiating the various stages of feeding behavior. The concept is covered extensively in the roosterfish chapter. Years of observation have brought me to the point of recognizing a progression of feeding activity starting with the curious non-feeder to the skeptical feeder, culminating with fish that aggressively attack the fly. It is interesting that this latter type of behavior may have actually delayed the development of some of the more consistent tactics that we now use. In other words on normal days I encountered fish that routinely followed and refused the fly leading me to think I was doing something wrong. And indeed part of the lack of catching was due to what I was or was not doing. When in truth, a lot of the reason the fish didn't strike had to do with the fish themselves.

Then along came the occasional very aggressive fish that savagely attacked the fly without hesitation. The message that I took away from this was that I finally did something miraculous. I had created a silver bullet on a hook or figured out the right twitch on retrieve. You know the type of event that inspires magazine articles about the new Secret Roosterfish Fly, or a new approach to stripping. Never mind that fish behavior had played a huge role in the outcome.

With this "success," I went out and repeated the new tactic again and again to each new fish encountered. The approach seemed logical to everyone but the fish. The simple reality was that I had found the hot fish willing to eat anything approximating a meal. Hindsight supports my current belief that the fish that display this feeding behavior are in an aggressive feeding mode and will take a number of retrieves and respond to a number of tactics. Unfortunately this type of feeding behavior is short lived and not encountered as often as we think it should.

In the case of roosterfish, I followed inconsistent tactics down the garden path when in reality they didn't work a majority of the time and for the majority of fish encountered. A good trout analogy to this, is fishing a hopper during a midge hatch, and finding one aggressive fish that eats the hopper. One can come away with the idea that hoppers are the solution to finicky trout during a micro hatch and continue to fish hoppers whenever a midge hatch is encountered. That can add up to a lot of missed opportunities on fish that could be caught with a better presentation of a midge pattern. The fly fisherman who sticks to the hopper may go a long time before finding another aggressive fish that eats outside the norm of fish behavior. I have found this to be the case with billfish, dorado, jacks and so forth. The world of saltwater fly fishing is still expanding in terms of our understanding of these magnificent fish and how to consistently catch them.

To begin this approach, let's look at what the fish feed on and the manner in which predators hunts their prey. In most cases the prey species consist of sardinas, mullet, ballyhoo, flying fish, mackerel and a host of other small fry. Imitating the size, shape, sonic imprint, action and color are critical, and were discussed in the chapter on fly selection and construction. The next step, is to take the fly and imitate bait fish behavior.

Think about trout fishing and the time and place to dead drift a nymph, swinging a soft hackle wet and strip a streamer. These are tactics that correlate to the activity of a specific food source and the corresponding fish feeding behavior. That doesn't mean that we don't swim some types of nymphs or don't dead drift a streamer. Indeed there are some instances when we change the retrieve in order to imitate the food source behavior. This approach is critical to catching saltwater predators as well.

The common prey species of interest to roosterfish, dorado, jacks and tunas are, for the most part, strong swimmers that seek protection from predation by forming into tight masses or bait balls. Failing that survival mode, it's a matter of either swim fast or die. Once a bait fish is forced out of the bait ball they never slow down while being pursued by the predator. Bait fish are often observed frantically swimming and leaping from the water in an effort to escape a stomach acid bathing party hosted by an even faster predator.

Should not our imitations swim in the same frantic manner as a bait fish in its attempt to escape imminent death? I have yet to witness any bait fish that would slow down or stop in front of their worst night mare. Although given the reaction of most predator fish to a fly that stops or slows down in front of them, that may just be the right escape tactic for a real sardina. Slowing down or pausing the presentation of the fly tends to reinforce the suspicion of a predator that this is not real food and should be avoided. The effect of slowing the retrieve in front of a fast swimming predator has the same effect of line drag while nymph or dry fly fishing for trout. Unless the trout are in super feed mode, they will refuse a poor presentation time and time again, as will our high speed saltwater predators.

From my vantage point as a guide, I can watch a fish's reaction to the strip of the fly and find a consistent pattern of refusal the instant the fly slows down or pauses in the strip. I find exception to this only during those times when the fish are in a frenzy of feeding activity. Lucky is the angler that happens upon a feeding bust (bust?) of roosters, tuna or dorado. The fishing can't get much easier. The unfortunate reality is that we spend most of our fishing time making presentations to fish that are not in an advanced state of feeding activity.

Understanding how predators feed is also important to how we present the fly. The majority of the blue water and inshore species that we pursue are fast swimmers that chase their prey down in order to eat them. Their approach to feeding is very different than the ambush feeders that lurk behind the reef waiting for an unsuspecting small fry to casually swim by. The roosters and dorado expect their prey to flee at mock speed and the retrieve should imitate that behavior. Tuna and jacks will also pursuit at high speed but, at times, will take advantage of cripples that result from predators ripping through the bait balls. In this instance, a dead drop presentation of the fly will imitate the cripples falling out.

The position that different species take around a bait ball will also influence the manner of presentation and retrieve. I have spent considerable time diving alongside bait balls, and certain patterns stand out to me. The bait fish themselves are fairly safe from attack while swimming in tight formation. But when a bait fish falls out from the mob they become susceptible to being quickly eaten. This can occur when they fail to follow the many turns and twists of the school or by predator fish blasting through the ball and scattering the bait fish.

All predators seem to exhibit this behavior. What is significant to us as fishermen is where the different species wait for the scattering to occur. Ladyfish, greenjacks and smaller roosters tend to wait at the bottom of the bait ball for an opportunity. The ideal presentation for them is to cast into the middle of the bait ball, let the fly sink through and out the bottom, then rip it as fast as possible away from the school. The bigger roosters and jacks tend to position closer to the surface to better use their broad body sides and in the case of the rooster, its comb, to herd the bait fish away from the school and attack them on the surface. Here a presentation to the top side edge of the school that moves parallel or away from the bait ball will tempt the larger roosters and jacks. This approach works well offshore for dorado, while sinking the fly through the bait ball followed by a rip works better for tuna.

Getting the Hookup

Understanding fish and bait behavior is the first part of the fish catching equation. The second part is taking that knowledge and presenting the fly in such a way as to elicit a strike by the target species. I divide this process into two parts; the first introduces the basic approach to presenting the fly, the second deals with the actual movement of the fly including stripping techniques, hand and rod movements.

Presentations that Work

There are three basic presentations of the fly that are commonly used with the many variations of movement applied. Two presentations are oriented to the surface; the third is intended to get the fly deeper in the water column.

The Intercept

The first presentation is often referred to in tarpon fishing as the intercept method, where the fly is cast at a shallow angle to the fish so that the fly is striped into the fish's view. The object of the presentation is to have fish and fly intersect each other in a way that doesn't threaten the fish. The angle of intercept varies by how spooky the fish are, how fast they are approaching, whether they are feeding on natural bait, and water clarity.

The ideal situation in all instances is when the fish is coming directly at you. In most cases, the fly should be presented between a 20 to 45 degree angle off of the path of the fish. In reference to a clock, if the fish is at 12:00, the presentation is between 1:00 and 2:00. A fly that lands directly behind the fish and comes up from behind will often spook the fish as will a fly coming at it from a 90 degree angle. In clock reference that would be from 3:00.

The intercept approach is most effective on the beach when the tide is low, the water is clear and the fish are spooky. I will encourage an angler to use an intercept presentation if they are slow in their ability to initiate the strip, in other words, inadvertently allowing the fly to settle in front of the fish. A fly presented off to the side and allowed to settle may not put the fish off as much as one allowed to pause after being presented right on its nose. I prefer deer hair heads on flies used in this fashion as they float on the surface much like a mullet that is loafing along the surface eating plankton. I have watched big roosters blast into whole schools of mullet feeding lazily upon the surface, apparently unaware of the approaching predator.

The intercept method has application on dorado schooled around the boat that has become wary to the fly. A few more fish in the school may respond better to a fly they intercept, rather than one that hits them on the nose. In the case of billfish, an intercept presentation is used to encourage a side-on strike of the fly so as to get a better hook up in the corner of the mouth. A fly engulfed by a billfish from directly behind very often results in the hook point partially buried in the roof of the mouth and is quickly expelled by the fish on the first jump.

The Direct Presentation

The second method of presentation is the direct approach. In this case, the fly is cast directly to and in front of the nose of the fish, and then quickly pulled away. This approach works best when the fish is focused on eating natural bait or is very excited by the action of a teaser. An essential key to making this approach work is applying movement to the fly immediately upon it entering the water. Wary fish, such as roosters, will recognize the fly as a fake if the imitation is given the chance to settle in the water before streaking off at high speed. This takes quick eye-hand coordination and lots of practice to grab the fly line as the fly is in air and start stripping as the fly enters the water. If this is difficult to achieve, the intercept approach is a better choice as any settling takes place out of direct view of the fish.

Under the right circumstances the direct approach leaves less room for casting error and allows you to make quicker presentations to excited and feeding fish. The direct approach is effective from the boat when teasing is used to arouse and move the fish into position. I also like the direct method on the beach in concert with a hook-less lure used as a teaser.

The Sink and Strip Presentation

The third method of presentation is to allow the fly to sink after the cast, then rip and strip it quickly back to the surface. This retrieve is designed to either imitate a cripple, or to sink the fly below the bait ball before pulling it out of the swimming mass of naturals. Along the beach the presentation to jacks and ladyfish may be a matter of letting the fly sink to a depth of six to ten feet. Yellowfin tuna working bait over a sea mount may require the fly reaching sixty feet of depth or more before the rip is applied. In either case, the fish may take during the drop, on the rip, or the retrieve back to the surface.

The Art of Stripping

The art of stripping compliments the method of presentation. The basic moves I will focus on here are the single-hand strip, the double-hand strip, as well as applied rod movements that we refer to as sweeps, rips or scissor strips. In discussing stripping methods it should be pointed out that some fly fishers are hardened advocates of either the single-hand or double-hand strip. I feel there are advantages and limitations to both methods and the savvy fisher knows when to employ either retrieve to their best advantage.

Single-Hand Strip

The most basic strip is the single-hand. It is familiar to all who have fished streamers to bass, trout, pike etc. To achieve the single hand strip, the fly is cast, the line placed under one or more fingers of the rod holding hand and the line pulled through the fingers by the other hand. In general, the cadence can be fast or slow, the strips long or short. For the species we encounter, this usually means stripping as fast and as long as you can, with a kick at the end of the strip. I know the speed is right if I feel a strain in the forearm and triceps of my stripping arm.

The single-hand strip goes well with the direct presentation, especially in short-cast situations, from the Panga and to teased fish. When using a direct presentation, I like to start the strip while the fly is still in the air. When done properly, the fly is moving the instant it hits the water while directly placed in front of the fish. This mitigates the problem of the fish seeing the fly settle in the water, a very unnatural thing for a bait fish to do in front of a predator. I liken this to throwing an in-the-air-mend to set up a drag-free drift for trout. This act is much easier and quicker for most fly casters to pull off while employing a single-hand retrieve. With practice, an in-the-air strip can be accomplished with the double-hand retrieve.

The advantage to the single-hand method is that the strip is easier to initiate quickly for many fishers. It still requires some practice and experience to make the cast and immediately pick up the line and begin stripping. Setting the hook and clearing line is less awkward from the single-hand position. Transition from the single-hand strip to a rod sweep is quicker, with less chance of allowing a pause in the retrieve.

The disadvantages of the single-hand strip are the pauses between strips. I have witnessed many a fish rush up to the fly only to turn off the instant the fly paused between hand strips. This can be offset somewhat by quicker hand movements.

Another trick is to apply a slight sweep of the rod between strips. It's a little like rubbing your head and patting your belly, but when accomplished, keeps the fly in constant motion. In all stripping methods, it is important to maintain a steady hold on the rod and not allow the tip of the rod to bounce every time the line is pulled by the stripping hand. The bouncing rod tip throws slack into the line and will accentuate the pause in the movement of the fly. I tend to place the rod tip just above the water and hold it there while stripping the fly. When casting from the beach, a fisherman can literally back up while retrieving to maintain a steady movement of the fly.

Double-Hand Strip

This method has gained popularity in recent years and is very popular on the East Coast for strippers and bluefish. After the cast is made, the butt section of the rod is placed under the armpit of the casting arm. Once the rod is securely in place, both hands are used to grip the line in sequence and pull the line in a hand-over-hand motion. I particularly like this stripping method for longer casts as is often the case on the beach. It works well for the intercept presentation as the cast is off to the side of the fish. This gives you time to pick up the line and start the strip without the fish scrutinizing a fly directly in front of its face.

The double hand works well for a drop presentation for the same reason, in that there is plenty of time to place the rod under the casting arm side, find the line in hand and prepare for the strip.

The third situation that plays well for the double-hand strip is when using a stripping basket. It is much easier to hit the basket hung on your waist with the shorter stroke of the two-handed retrieve.

The advantages to using the double-hand strip lie in both line speed and consistent movement of the fly during the retrieve, and the keys to getting hook ups. But, they are not the only elements necessary to sell the fly and get a strike rather than a follow and last-minute refusal. Remember that one of the themes to this chapter is to differentiate between the two responses by the fish and what we must do to get the strike.

The disadvantages to the double hand have to do as much with the experience and skill of the angler as they do with the method. Most of the disadvantages can be overcome with practice and time on the water. The first challenge to using the double-hand strip is the time it takes to place the rod under the arm, gather up the line and begin the strip. This is critical when casting directly to the fish and any pause could indicate that the fly is a fraud. The second point of difficulty with the double-hand occurs at the end of the retrieve when trying to impart a scissor strip or sweep of the rod. The transition time of removing the rod from under the armpit to the hand can create a pause in the movement of the fly. The third disadvantage of note, is in setting the hook with the rod under the arm. For the newly-initiated this can be an awkward moment. Time and practice can smooth out this operation as well.

I personally like to use the double-hand strip where I can, with an appreciation for what it can do in terms of hooking fish. My word of caution here is to be aware of the consequences of misfires while stripping. I remember a conversation with a fisherman on the beach who liked the double-hand because he got a lot more fish to follow the fly. He hadn't caught any yet, but he was having fun in the attempt. Keep in mind that fish that follow are exciting but the more important factor is the ability to get the fish to eat the fly. A pause in the movement of the fly due to missing the line by the stripping hand, a slow transition in and out of the arm pit can be the deciding factor of whether the fish refuses at the end of an exciting follow or if the fish eats the fly. In this respect, the single-hand strip is a good starting point as it is easier to learn and less likely to muff at the critical time. I encourage you to work on your skills with both stripping methods to develop a good double-hand retrieve.

Rips, Scissor Strips and Rod Sweeps

Rips, scissor strips and rod sweeps are the exclamation point in presentation that can make the difference between a hook up versus a fish that only follows. By a rod sweep, I mean moving the rod parallel to the water in a manner that accelerates the movement of the fly in a way that imitates the escape mode of a bait fish. The speed of the sweep is just under the point that the fly skitters on the surface. The scissor strip simply adds a hand strip at the end of sweep, thus extending the distance of the presentation. A rip is a fast lift on the rod when presenting the fly deep.

When applied at the right moment, any of these tactics can trigger the strike reaction on the part of the target fish. To them it appears that the bait fish is trying its best to escape. A typical strip and sweep cadence on a short cast to a teaser is three to four hard strips followed by a sweep and or scissor strip. The sweep transitions into a roll cast at the end of the retrieve to lift the fly up and out of the water. You are then able to re-present the fly to the fish that followed, or cast to other fish working the teaser. When blind casting from the beach, I tend to make more strips due to the longer casts involved, but always end with a sweep in case a fish I can't see is rushing out of the froth to eat my fly. In either case, once the fish turns on the fly, I make the transition from stripping to an immediate sweep of the rod. The longer the fish follows a straight up strip of either the single- or double-hand variety, the greater the chance the fish will refuse at the end of all your efforts. The sweep or scissor strip is the reality trigger that gets the fish to eat.

Roll Cast and Sweep

The roll cast is a basic casting method that has an important place in saltwater fishing. The distances encountered while fishing to teased fish from the boat are usually well within the range of a roll cast. This method incorporates a rod sweep as soon as the fly hits the water. The speed of the fly is much faster than what we can achieve with a hand strip, and there is no pause in fly movement during the retrieve. No other method can present the fly in as fast a manner or with as many repetitions as the roll and sweep. I use it on the beach when the rooster or jacks are busting bait in the wave trough. The water is teeming with thousands of fleeing bait fish, the water is frothy and the feeding is frantic. It can take a lot of casts in a short period of time in order to get a hook up. The quick succession of roll casts and sweeps increases the percentages in our favor. The roll and sweep is very effective for dorado blasting bait fish close to the boat.

The roll cast safely allows the fisher to work on crowded decks by avoiding overhead obstacles, fellow anglers and crew. Roll casting allows more than one angler to get into the action when a school of fish is pounding bait near the boat. Roll casting is also easier on the body, especially when you switch back and forth between a conventional forward cast and the roll cast during the day.

Wind is the bane of the seas and can shut down our ability to cast accurately, if at all. When the wind comes up while pulling teasers, we head the bow into the wind and roll cast from the stern. Anyone with a little practice can lay out forty to fifty feet of line on a roll cast with the wind at their back. And, the Captain and I are a lot less likely to wear a streamer fly earring when clients are roll casting in windy situations.

The disadvantages to roll and sweep is the limited distance the fly can be cast and retrieved compared to what a good caster can accomplish with a conventional forward cast. Another concern is the rod position at the end of the retrieve can end up too far above and behind youwhich will affect your ability to set the hook. Roll casting can lead to high sticking on the hook set, which in turn, results in broken rods.

Chumming and Teasing

Excluding flats fishing, the practice of chumming and teasing is as much a part of saltwater fly fishing as strike indicators are a part of nymph fishing. There are times and places where chumming and teasing are not necessary and even times when either tactic can be counterproductive. Both tactics are key tools in our ability to attract, hold in place and catch saltwater species. The ocean is a huge place to find game fish with no guarantees that once located they can be held close enough or long enough to make a presentation. Chum and teasers can greatly help set the table to the angler's advantage.

Chumming

Chum comes live or dead, chunked, chopped puréed or liquefied. On the Baja, the preference is strongly in favor of live flatiron herring or locally known as sardinas. They are abundant, available and have long been the mainstay with the local Captains. There have been times when the sardinas have disappeared for periods of time and we have been forced into innovative means to attract and hold fish.

It was after one such fall period when the sardinas went elsewhere that partner John and I decided we needed to take things in our own hands and make our own chum. So, on the next trip down, a large hand grinder went into my checked bag. We were going to take advantage of the pesky meedlefish and the many filleted-out carcasses around the fish shack to make some chum. The first evening back at the hotel, John and I, armed with my grinder and a supply of beer, headed down to the fish-cleaning shack to grind us some chum. We were dismayed to find a platoon of wild cats making off with our chum stock. Dropping beer and grinder, we charged off into a Baja thorn field to rescue our carcasses. In short order we emerged sweaty and bloodied, but with enough dorado and tuna leftovers to test our new machine. We set up amongst the flies and ambiance of the cleaning shack and started cutting and grinding. All we got was mush; turns out my garage sale special lacked the necessary cutting blades. An hour of grimy work produced about a quart of fish mush and a resolve to find another way. To add insult to injury, the bottle of chum we put in the freezer was thrown out by one of the kitchen staff before we ever got a chance to use it.

Despite the lack of a good blade, I took the grinder on board the boat the next day to grind up some of the all too available needlefish that plagued us that year. In a gruesome reenactment of the movie *Fargo*, I placed the tail of a needlefish into the grinder and started cranking the long skinny body through to the head. The act grossed out the very nice couple on board and resulted in needlefish mush of little use.

The next trip down, John brought a light-duty blender, another garage sale special. We were temporarily quartered in the hotel owner's house, so we set up shop in the kitchen with the blender and a bag of dead sardinas. The little herring proved too much for the blender and it died a violent death in the kitchen sink. Little did we know that several chunks must have found their way into the p-trap under the sink. We surmised as much after the house keeper made note of a bad smell coming from the kitchen. We had since moved to our normal room and hadn't detected it before leaving. We did a good job of playing dumb about the smell.

On the next trip down, John came armed with an industrial size Cuisinart. I brought a case of canned fish flavored cat food and that is what we occasionally use today when the sardinas take a hike for parts unknown.

Dead chum in its various forms and consistencies is a great attractant to reef species such as pargo, triggerfish, cabrilla and snapper. The cat food mixed in with chunks of skipjack or sardina is a dinner bell seldom ignored by such species. Whole dead sardinas can attract feeding hordes of ladyfish, dorado, yellowfin tuna, jack crevalle, pompano, the reef species, along with a host of others. When throwing whole sardinas into the chum line, we cast Clouser minnows and fish them on the dead drop. Most takes come on the fall, although some fish will hit the fly on the retrieve. Almost all tropical Pacific species will respond to dead chum with the exception of the roosterfish. I have seen some exceptions to this, but for the most part, they prefer their food in fine swimming form.

In recent years we have taken to packing dead sardinas or chunked skipjack into a two-inch PVC pipe with holes drilled into the cap and a plug at the end of the tube. Two nine-inch squid squirts are zip-tied to the tube and the whole thing is trolled 25 feet behind the boat as a smelly teaser. Dorado, sailfish and striped marlin love the thing.

Live chum is still the mainstay in the Sea of Cortez, mainly in the form of the flatiron herring or sardina. Nothing pulls game fish like the real live thing.

But too much of a good thing can have a detrimental effect. When there is too much chum in the water the fish have a choice of what they eat and will often ignore the fly in favor of the real thing. Live chum can also pull catchable fish away from the fly. Many a time I have watched a fish charge a fly only to turn off at the last instant to chase some freshly-tossed sardinas. The key with live chum is to put enough in the water to bring on the fish and hold them, but not so many that the fly is ignored. Two sardinas tossed to four roosterfish plus the fly equates to a good chance that competition among the fish will result in a hook up.

Live Teasers

Live bait teasing is one of the greatest tools in our arsenal and can be applied to about any saltwater species found from the Sea of Cortez on down to the Equator. It is especially important in seducing big roosters. Most of the true grands our clients have caught have come from live bait teasing.

We use live bait on a teasing rod to work reluctant billfish into a feeding mode along with dorado, amberjack, crevalles and wahoo. The teaser can be presented by trolling at very slow speed or by casting. Quite often we locate the schools by slow trolling, then switch to casting to specific fish in the school.

The type of bait used is critical. First of all, it has to be lively and fresh. Bait kept overnight in receiver nets are stressed and short lived in the bait tank the following day. Making your own bait ensures fresh bait, but does cut into fishing time. In many of the places I have fished up and down the coast of Mexico and Central America, we caught our bait. On the East Cape, the tradition has changed to buying bait from local vendors. This is the result of a program to move commercial net fishermen into the sport fishing industry in order to protect the fishery. I support that move and gladly pay for bait. Besides it gets us on the water quicker. I do my business whenever possible with the Sardineros who have fresh bait.

Not all bait species are equal when it comes to teasing. The best baits swim on the surface where we can see them, have good endurance on the teasing line and in the live well. Caballitos, greenjacks, and blue runners are available up and down the tropical Pacific Coast, are tough, long-lived swimmers and game fish love them. They do not make good teaser baits for the simple reason that they swim too deep. It's mighty hard to tease a fish you can't see because they are locked onto a bait swimming deep. Mackerel swim on top, but are not long lived in the tank and tire easily in the water. My choice for live bait is herring/sardina, and mullet. The larger sardinas can be acquired in enough quantity to throw as free swimming chum and appeal to many medium sized fish. If freshly caught, they last in the live well and have reasonable hang time on the line. They are tops for small to medium roosters. There are times of the year however when only small sardinas, less than three inches, are available. They are much more fragile than their bigger brothers and are a better free swimming chum fish then a rigged teaser at that size.

The mullet is great teaser bait and hands down my favorite for big roosters, dorado and billfish. They are a tough species that swim on top of the water where they can be controlled in front of a game fish. They out last about anything in the bait tank and are common to most warm waters. Mullet are tough enough to allow a rooster to mouth the bait and pull it away repeatedly without killing it. I have seen many a mullet all but completely scaled by fish attacks and still have the strength to swim.

Tackle and Rigging for Live Teasers

My preference for a teasing stick is a spinning rod eight to nine feet long with a soft tip. The reel should have a high rate of retrieve and loaded with spectra line. To this I add

25 or 30 lb. mono line as a top shot. The line is threaded through a plastic bubble (think fly and a bubble here), and secured by a San Diego knot attached to a coast lock swivel. The bubble serves several purposes. You can always find the location where the bait is swimming and get on target quickly. Knowing where the bait is, helps you to avoid crossing your fly line over the teasing rod line. The bubble inhibits the tendency of the bait to swim off to one side or the other of the boat making shots at approaching fish more difficult. The bubble serves as a target with a built-in three-foot lead. This tends to result in more casts placed in front of the fish especially if the bait is being pulled rapidly towards the boat.

To the swivel below the bubble, I attach a three- to four-foot fluorocarbon leader with a loop knot. The business end of the leader is attached to a snap large enough to clip across the nose of the sardina, or up through the top lip of small mullet. A small circle hook, size two or smaller can also be used, though incidental hook ups will occur with aggressive fish. The advantage to using a hook is that it is faster to replace the bait when the action gets crazy and fish are stripping the teaser bait off the rig. When rigging larger mullet, I like to sew a loop of floss through their nose and clip the loop of floss to the snap. It is best to have three or four baits rigged and ready to go for when the action picks up and a quick change is needed. Brightly colored floss is helpful to quickly locate the rigged baits in the tanks, especially if it is also full of sardinas.

Fishing to a Teaser

Teasing is a team effort of Captain, teaser and fisher. The concept is simple, put the fly on the fish chasing the teaser. The mechanics are the challenge. The keys to success are:

The cast must come quickly and on target before the fish looses interest or is able to make off with the bait.

Cast in front of the fish.

Presentations to the side or behind the teaser seldom result in hook ups with roosters. Other species can be more forgiving.

Lead the teaser by shortening up the cast. Keep in mind that the teaser is a moving target. The person handling the teasing rod is quite often reeling like crazy to keep the bait from being eaten by an aggressive fish. And quite often, the cast falls too long as the distance to the teaser closes up fast with frantic reeling. Roosters do not like having the fly come scooting up their backside. That is just not natural to them.

Focus your presentations on the teaser regardless of other feeding activity around you. It is tempting to make casts to other fish feeding around the boat. The problem is that if you cast to a bust, the fish is already gone looking for the next natural bait. The teaser controls the position of the fish and holds them there longer, giving the fly a chance to fall into place. Most hook ups will come within three feet of the teaser.

Increase the speed of retrieve as soon as the fish turns on the fly. Be aware that the really aggressive fish will eat regardless of speed changes, but they are the exception. My advice is to treat every fish as a finicky feeder and put a sweep into the retrieve sooner than later. The longer the fish follows behind the fly, the great the chance they will refuse at the end of the retrieve.

Don't waste time retrieving all the way to the boat when there is lots of activity around the teaser. The time spent retrieving all the way in takes away from time the fly is in play next to the teaser. Make three of four hard strips; sweep the fly with the rod and quickly cast back to the teaser.

Teasing with Lures

Hook-less plugs make great teasers and are a blast to work for the benefit of the person casting the fly. I get as much of a kick out of throwing the teaser as I do throwing the fly. We use hook-less lures to attract and excite many of the species we target such as roosterfish, jacks, tuna, skipjacks, billfish, pargo, snappers and snook.

I keep a good selection of top water plugs, shallow running crank baits and soft plastic swim baits in my kit bag at all times. The basic concept of use and presentation are much the same as using live bait for a teaser. Both techniques attract and excite fish while placing the fish in an ideal position to present the fly. Lures can compliment live bait teasing too. I will often throw a hook-less lure from the boat while a mullet or sardina is swimming tethered behind.

The idea is to draw fish close enough to encounter the live teaser. Lures are a great way to bring schools of dorado to the boat, then throw live chum into the water to hold them with in casting range. This can be highly effective with fish encountered on the troll, dorado holding under debris or spotted swimming on the surface. We had a spectacular day for dorado in Costa Rica throwing teasers at floating trash caught in the current seams. The Captain moved the boat slowly down the seam and I would throw the plug to the bigger piles of debris. The dorado slashed wildly at the plug, following it into fly casting range of the client. Many hook ups resulted from this effort and a good time was had by all.

Surface Plugs

Surface plugs are my favorite teasing lure for several reasons, the first being that they are very effective in gaining a reaction from most game fish. The slashing and gurgling of a surface plug is a dinner bell that game fish pick up at considerable distance. It is much easier to visually follow the approach of the game fish following a floating lure and make any necessary adjustments to the speed and action of the tease. You can likewise pick up the movement and progress of the fish following the lure. Fish that are teased up on floating plugs are also more inclined to hit fly rod poppers. Top water action really pegs the fun meter for me.

My favorite lures include four to five inch cigar shaped bass plugs for smaller roosters and jacks. I like them when a more subtle approach is called for, such as low and clear water conditions. A quick walk-the-dog or fast skitters will draw lots of action.

The standard teaser on the beach is the Robert Lure line including Rangers and Whistlers. These plugs were designed for stripers and bluefish along the East Coast and eventually migrated to the Baja and tropical Pacific beyond. They can be worked on the surface with a fast skitter or allowed to sink. I almost always fish them on the surface. The weight and design of the lure is ideal for the beach, as you can cast it a mile with spectra line thus reaching out to the more distant cruising fish.

Chuggers, poppers, pencil poppers and pop bottle lures create a tremendous amount of surface commotion and attract game fish from the furthest distances. They work well for aggressive roosters, jacks, dorado and members of the tuna family. Watching sailfish blow up on a Yo-Zuri Bull is an unforgettable experience. These lures can be popped, skittered or finessed in a walk-the-dog fashion. However you work it, the most effective retrieve for teasing is fast.

Crank Baits

Shallow running crank baits are a good alternative to the surface plugs when a good chop is on the water or when the fish seem to be shying off of the commotion created by the poppers. The main disadvantage to using crank baits is that they are harder for the fly caster to visually pick up as they are retrieved. The fish behavior is also harder to read if they are following the lure below the water surface. Add glare to the situation and it becomes even harder to tell if the fish is still on track or not. I tend to keep my cast shorter with crank baits then I do with surface plugs so that the fly caster can track them better and making the fish behavior easier to observe, if the action is kept closer to the boat.

Swim Baits

We picked up some large soft plastic swim baits at a show several years ago as a hedge against days when live bait was unavailable. Sure enough, partner John had one of those early season days when the bait suppliers couldn't get out due to rough seas. He trolled the swim bait behind the boat in the same manner that we do with live bait. The tally for the day was seven large jacks and three nice roosterfish. The swim baits come out whenever we run out of live bait and have served us well.

Smaller wiggle tails, slugs and such have proven effective when cast from the boat, beach or kayak.

Presentation of the fly is the key to catching more fish. Good tackle, knots well tied, and the hot fly play a part, but in the greater scheme of things, it is the presentation of the fly that makes the difference.

In this chapter I began the discussion of fish behavior and differentiated between feeders and followers and how we can turn the follower to a feeder. I will pick up this theme again in the chapter on roosterfish, and expand it into a description of the different feeding stages one can observe and use to adjust teasing and stripping techniques. The stages of feeding behavior would fit perfectly into this chapter on presentation. They are so key to success with roosterfish, that I decided to put that discussion in the roosterfish chapter. Stages of feeding behavior can be applied to many, if not all, species we encounter on the Baja and beyond. Roosterfish being the toughest to fool, are the best example to use to illustrate the concept for all the other species.

Photograph by Brian O'Keefe

Photograph by the author

6

After the Hook Up: Keeping Them on Without Busting Your Tackle or Your Knuckles

I debated whether to include a section on fighting fish in this book until I got to thinking about the number of rods that we see broken each season and the number of fish that break off; both unhappy circumstances that usually occur on the first big fish hooked on the trip. The memory of the fish fighting provides the lesson of the day before can scrambled by the flush of emotion that comes with hooking a good fish.

These saltwater species are incredibly strong for their size and capable of sudden bursts of speed that can catch even veteran fishermen off guard, resulting in broken leaders and occasionally a shattered rod.

To limit the potential of broken equipment, it is important to be aware of the most common causes of tackle melt down and, as much as possible, eliminate the factor of human error. I don't always think that human error is a bad thing either, broken rods aside. This is a challenging experience, full of adrenaline-charged emotion and stuff does occur in the excitement of the moment. In the end it is sometimes the fish that got away that is the one most remembered.

In this chapter, I will take you through the course of events from hook up to landing discussing fish-fighting techniques, pointing out the potential pit falls at each stage, and reinforcing the remedies.

Setting the Hook

The most common error that fresh water fly fishermen and especially trout fly fishermen make while setting the hook, is to give it the old high stick. This makes good sense for trout as we are using flexible rods, small sharp hooks and are dealing with slack line that needs to be eliminated quickly. In the salt, a high candy cane bend does little to drive a large hook into the tough mouth of big fish. Worse yet, the rod can shatter in a micro second when bent at that angle.

Some of the toughest folks to cure this habit of, are trout guides. I remember a trip when four trout-guide friends of ours came down to sample the best of the Baja. First cast, first hook up, first high stick and one rod down was the start of the trip. By the end of the week, six rods were headed back to the manufacture for replacement, and the cure was still not in place for at least one of the trout guides. Some habits are highly ingrained.

The proper hook set for big saltwater species is a strip set coupled with a low rod angle to the fish. In most cases, we are stripping line at a high rate of speed and the fish is striking at an even higher rate of speed, so taking up slack is seldom an issue. A sweep of the rod to the side, but never more than a 45 degree angle to the fish, and a smooth pull with the stripping hand is all that it takes to come tight on the fish. Big roosters and billfish may require an additional jab to ensure that the hook is seated into their hard mouths.

This is, of course, assuming that the hook the fly is built on, is a J-hook. For flies tied on circle hooks, you simply have to come tight on the fish and the rest is taken care of by hook design and physics. Most of my billfish flies are tied on circle hooks and I find the hook up rate is higher, especially with anglers new to the game.

Too Hot to Handle, the First Two Minutes

After a good hook set, the next two or so minutes are the most critical. A lot can happen to break a fish off during the initial crazy run of a big dorado, rooster, tuna or billfish. A little pre-planning and preparation can alter the outcome in your favor. Take care to survey your surroundings before even casting to a fish. Note if there are exposed cleats, water separator filters, equipment or other objects that can catch the fly line during the initial run of the fish. Without a doubt, the biggest dorado I ever hooked, broke off when the slack line wrapped around the railing on the boat.

Take note of your feet. Are you standing on your line? I go barefoot on the boat to be able to feel the line under my feet. As the guide, the last place I want to be is on top of the client's line when Old Moe is outward bound. The same barefoot advice is applicable to you. Be forewarned. Experience has taught me that the person casting to a big fish is fairly often unaware of their feet at that moment. I find that I can feel the line under foot when I am guiding, but due to mission focus when I am fishing, my feet become insensitive clubs. My advice is to use your eyes to check where your feet are, along with the other boat hazards.

Part of your pre-planning is to check the length of line that you have coiled at your feet. It should be no more than your average cast. Too much line lying around seems to find something to attach itself to. I recently shared the boat with a good fly caster who had a tendency to strip off too much line in anticipation of the need for a longer cast. I mentioned this to him and he shortened up for a while. Eventually several long casts had left an excess of line on the deck coincidental to me teasing a monster bull dorado right up to the boat. The cast was short, the slack was long and the strike was smashing. In a heartbeat, the fish was catapulting itself for some distant horizon while the slack line curled up and around the reel seat and fighting butt of the rod. I saw it all happen, helpless to be more than a witness in anticipation of hearing the leader snap. But no snap ensued, just the graceful arched launch of rod and reel into the deep blue. I gave it my best shot by diving overboard after the rod, but I swim a lot slower than the pokiest dorado and that rod and reel is still out there somewhere.

Setting the Drag

At this point I get a bit controversial. There are two schools of thought on the use and setting of drag during the fight with a large fish on a direct drive reel. One approach is to start with a light drag setting of four or five pounds and incrementally increasing the pressure at different stages of the fight. The alternative method is to set the drag in the four to six pound range and leave it alone for the duration of the fight. All the drag pressure is created by palming the rim of the reel and pinching the line against the cork handle. There is a time and place for both approaches, as well as a combination of techniques. My views are somewhat biased by my experience as a fishing guide, witnessing the full range of experience and skill levels of my clients. Experience and skill level is definitely a factor in how drag is applied on a fly reel.

Along sandy beaches and in the blue water realm where I spend most of my time, I have become an advocate for the later approach. This assumes two things: one that you are using a direct drive reel and two that you are not about to be spooled or tangled in rocks, roots or anchor lines. In an attempt to either stop or lose a fish, I most assuredly advocate cranking the drag down to the max. Once the danger has passed, I advocate that you back off the drag and continue the fight by palming the reel. Otherwise, the less you fiddle with the drag, the less chance for bad things to happen. As a saltwater guide and avid fisherman, I have witnessed (and participated in) bad things happening after a drag is tightened down during the fight. The common scenario is that the fish eventually tires and comes easily to the boat only to revive and burst away, leaving you a mere split second to react and loosen the drag. The result can range from a perfect adjustment to a broken leader, broken rod, or conversely, a free spool mess. The person palming the reel or pinching the line during the fight has only to let go of line or spool and the fish is pulling against a nice smooth light drag. Yes, the fish is going to gain some line initially, but the run is usually short at this point and they are expending a lot of energy in the process. Patience at this point in the fight will put the fish in the boat quicker in the end.

How much pressure can you exert with palming a spool? My research indicates that you can achieve twelve to fourteen pounds of pressure. That, added to line drag in the water, and you can quickly come up to the breaking point of most class tippets. Besides the ability to make quicker adjustments to the drag tension, palming reduces the degree of friction on the drag disk and torque on the reel frame. A good saltwater fly reel will last a life time when used this way. Our reels see at least a hundred days of use a year. I have many reels that are six to eight years old that still use the same drag disk they came with.

When do you start to pressure the fish? On the initial run of a large fish I usually let the fish run unabated against the drag with no palming until I start to feel the fish begin to slow down. At that point I begin to slowly apply pressure to the spool, gradually increasing the pressure till the fish stops. This all goes out the window if the fish shows no sign of slowing and is on track to empty the spool. Then is the time to crank down on the drag dial, hang on and think about the knot connection to your arbor. Ditto this action if your quarry is headed for an entanglement of rocks, roots and anchor lines. Getting spooled actually doesn't happen that often unless you pick a fight with a big fish on significantly undersized tackle. Forty pounds of panicked dorado and a 100 meter spool of backing is asking for a test of your arbor knot. My guess is that you will be wondering quite soon how to replace the fly line and backing as well. Big blue marlin have given us some hellacious rides deep into the spools of our largest capacity reels. Discretion upon hook up is called for here by initiating a quick break off to prevent spooling.

There is a down side to palming and that is your fingers are closer to the whirling blur of the reel handle as the fish is taking line. Bruised knuckles can result if you are not careful. The way to avoid a collision with the reel handle is to keep your fingers tight together and not cup the reel in your hand. In other words keep the palm of your hand flat, fingers tight to each other and no cupping.

Relying on palm pressure may not create enough drag pressure in some situations. When fishing for pargo and cabrilla around the rocks, big jacks around anchored boats come to mind in my back yard. If you are headed for an encounter with giant trevalles around coral heads, snook or tarpon in the mangroves then tight drag adjustments are an important tool.

If you are not comfortable with palming a reel and wish to utilize the drag to its fullest extent, then I suggest that you look for a reel with a large drag adjustment dial. The adjustment should be a matter of a few well-defined clicks between light to heavy pressure. The more you have to turn the drag dial to tighten or loosen the drag, the greater the chance of breaking off a fish. The next step is to get very familiar with the drag range on the reel in order to make the proper adjustment during the fight. Better yet is to look beyond a direct drive reel. There are a number of manufacturers that make fly reels that work like a conventional reel with gears, clutches and drags systems designed to work like a conventional reel. The disadvantage is weight, cost and the inability to use palming as an alternative.

Rod Positions

Rule number one here is to never high stick the rod. It does little to pressure the fish and greatly increases the chance of breaking the rod. As a general rule of thumb, the rod should never exceed a 45 degree angle of position to the fish, regardless of whether the angle is up or laid to the side. Beyond that point the rod is susceptible to breakage as well as exceeding any further ability to increase pressure on the fish. In other words the rod is maxed out in its ability to apply pressure or lift.

During the initial run of the fish I like to maintain enough of a rod angle to absorb any sudden jerks. The rest of the pressure comes directly off of the drag on the reel and a shallow rod bend. An angle of 20 degrees is a good starting point. As the fish begins to tire on its first run, increase the rod angle to 45 degrees. Greater rod angle can usually be employed through the rest of the fight. As the fish is brought closer to the boat or beach, low side angles can be used to great effect on the fish. Changing rod angles pulls on different muscle groups, thus tiring the fish quicker. A different rod angle may also move a fish that has been effectively sulking and immoveable.

Proper Pumping

Once the fish quits running, it is time to take maximum advantage and gain line as quickly as possible. Smaller fish and long skinny fish can be often reeled in directly. Be ready to let go of the reel handle if the fish suddenly revives and take off again. However, if the fish is large and resists coming in by reel pressure alone, it is time to start pumping. The idea is to move the fish toward you by lifting the rod and retrieving the line onto the reel when the rod is lowered.

There are several key points to gaining the maximum amount of line back on the reel. The first is to start your rod lift as low as you can, most cases being at water level, then lifting all the way to a 45 degree angle. The second key is to start reeling immediately as you lower the rod. Many beginners don't start gaining line until the rod is half way down to its starting point. That equates to a lot of heavy lifting in a hot tropical sun with little effect to reward your efforts. The next key is to not pause between lifts. Keep pumping as long as you can move the fish or have the strength to continue. When you rest, the fish can rest, and that will prolong the fight, bad for you and bad for the fish.

Short Stroke

After the first long run, most fish will give to the pressure of the long stroke and allow you to gain line back onto the reel. Smaller fish may be landed fairly quickly after the first big run. Larger fish, however, will usually revive enough to turn sideways to the pressure of the rod and seemingly become an immoveable object. If allowed to sit and hold, the fish will eventually revive enough to make another long run or simply conserve enough energy to make the battle an epic adventure.

This is not a time to rest. You can still take the fight to the fish with a tactic called the short stroke. Begin the rod lift at water level and lift the rod to the point that it stops bending. If there is no give whatsoever on the fish, back off a little and try a different angle. Try the lift again and take any line that you can get from the fish, but never exceed the point that the rod stops bending.

Quickly reel in the line that you just gained. This is called short stroke because the length of stroke is shortened due to the resistance of the fish. However, some small amount of line can often be gained. Even if it is just inches gained, you are at least moving the fish and forcing it to expend more energy than what it wants to at that time. Quick, smooth strokes in short succession should be applied as long as you can feel any give on the part of the fish. If the fish is truly large and truly immoveable back off and simply maintain pressure till the fish moves. In this case, plan on being there for a while.

Many anglers up against their first big fish fear breaking the fish off and back down on the pressure or rest too long between strokes when they could be moving the fish. Even light tippets can take a lot of pressure in the form of a steady pull. Sudden jerks on the part of fish or fisherman are the more likely to break the leader. The longer the fight goes on, the greater the odds are in favor of the fish breaking off due to leader abrasion or the hook wearing a larger hole and slipping free of its hold on the fish's mouth.

Close to the Boat, Tip to Tail

There are several rod maneuvers that you can perform to apply pressure and shorten the time taken to land a large fish. A commonly used tactic is often referred to as "Tip to Tail." The idea here, is to change the angle of pull against the fish and force it to use different muscles, thus expend more energy and shortening the duration of the fight. This tactic works only when the fish is close to the boat, otherwise the angle of pull against the fish with a lot of line still out is negligible.

To perform the move, simply move the rod tip to where it is pointing at the tail of the fish as it swims perpendicular to you. In other words, if the fish is swimming across left to right, move the rod to the left and behind the direction the fish is moving. Point the rod tip at its tail. If the fish responds to the new pressure and turns the opposite direction, smoothly swing the rod to the right and point it at the tail. In this way the fish is getting pressure from both the side and from the rear. Some species such as dorado and billfish will respond by jumping upon feeling the change in direction of pull. This is a plus given the energy the fish must expend in order to clear the water. It also provides great photo opportunities and garners oohs and aahs from the spectators.

Down and Dirty

After several tip to tail maneuvers and when the fish has settled down, it is time to press the fight to the next level. The next move is called "down and dirty." It begins like a tip to tail in that the rod moves from the head to the tail of the fish. To perform a down and dirty, continue moving the rod past the tail of the fish until you completely roll the fish over. To gain the most affect, the fish should be in the later stage of resistance. Timed right, the maneuver upsets the fish's equilibrium and can leave them spent and disoriented. Immediately following a successful tip to tail maneuver is an opportune time to grab leader or tail and finish the fight. When applied too early, a hot fish may go into panic mode by leaping or attempting to run. If the fish doesn't break off, you have accomplished something in getting the fish to expend more energy.

In the absence of these maneuvers, the fight can enter into a prolonged slug fest where the fish swims back and forth with enough resistance to keep from being landed, all the while conserving its energy. The fight can go on forever, or so it seems in a hot tropical sun. Dorado, jack crevalle and roosterfish all have broad sides that they can effectively and efficiently leverage against the line of pull while expending minimal energy. It is important for the sake of a fish you wish to release and your own well being to press the attack on the fish and fight as aggressively as the tackle allows.

Moment of Truth, the Landing

At last the fish is spent and it is time to prepare for the landing and hopefully a Kodak moment. The fish is now alongside the boat, the fly line is reeled up so that the leader is just outside of the tip guide, and the fish is vanquished.

What do you do? For one, please don't reel the leader into the guides. The prettiest knots can still hang in the guides and create havoc if the fish decides "it ain't over till the fat fisher sings." Instead place the rod tip over the guide's shoulder and back to the opposite side of the boat. The guide/mate will slide his or her hand down the leader and handle the fish. Standing in place and lifting the fish will result in a broken leader, or worse, a broken rod. Once the fish is secured by the mate, give them some slack line to work with. Now take a deep breath, relax, shoot some pictures and get the fish back in the water if that is your intent. If you wish to keep the fish for dinner the same process applies. Step back, let the mate gaff the fish, then give them some slack line. Check your leader and knots for fraying. If you just landed a large fish, the safest course of action is to cut the fly off with the last three inches of leader and re-tie. This can be hard to do when the dorado are busting bait around the boat. Now go get another.

Photograph by Brian O'Keefe

Photograph by Brian O'Keefe

7

Roosterfish:
Baja's Rock Star and Greatest Challenge on the Fly

The roosterfish truly speaks to the soul of fly fishing the on the Baja, recently rising to almost rock star status. Pez gallo is unique in its appearance with its tall rooster like comb, striking black on white markings as well as its elusive, though at times, aggressive behavior.

In my research, I found very little biological information on roosterfish. My reading indicates a general agreement among the fishery biologists that the roosterfish is in the jack family. Their appearance, feeding behavior and fighting style are reminiscent of the jack crevalle. It is at the genus, species level that the biologist diverge in opinion as to how close the roosterfish is to the rest of the jack family. Little is known about their migration and reproduction habits. One tagging study is being conducted in Costa Rica at this time. I am looking forward to reading the results.

Roosterfish were long considered impossible to catch on the fly and they continue to befuddle the best of fly fishermens' efforts. Their feeding behavior runs the gamut from highly aggressive to extremely selective, seeming to transition from one mode to the other in a fin stroke. Many anglers have compared the roosterfish to the permit for its ability to baffle the angler and reject our best offerings. There are definitely days when the comparison bears relevance. As with the permit, we have learned ways to tip the scale in our favor, and when conditions are right, we can fool this magnificent marauder of the beaches of the Baja. Unlike the permit on the flats, there are short time periods when the rooster drops its cautious feeding pattern and goes on a tear, hitting natural bait and the fly with near abandon. The lucky few who have experienced this can be seduced into the belief they have found the magic fly or technique only to face days and weeks of frustration and rejection. This is a fish that can instill humility while firing the imagination with keen anticipation of the next encounter. I have been through this cycle so many times, thinking that somehow I had found a magic bullet only to be reminded that on most days the rooster is one tough challenge on the fly. Happily along the way, a pattern of feeding behavior has emerged, revealing tactics and techniques for hooking this game fish on a more consistent basis.

The feeding mode of the roosterfish follows a progression with identifiable behaviors in respect to response to natural food in the water, live teaser and artificial fly. The ability to read fish behavior, relative to the stage of feeding aggression, is important to applying a tactical approach that will catch the roosterfish. Good trout fishermen understand this approach and know that trout feeding on aquatic insects follows a progression based on food source activity. On a typical trout fishing day, we start the morning with a deep drift of a nymph imitation prior to the initial hatch activity, as the natural insects begin to unhook from the bottom and drift freely in the current. We observe movement of the fish intercepting the bugs and often see a flash of white as the fish opens its mouth. As the hatch progresses and the insects begin to move towards the surface, we observe that the fish are suspended higher in the water column. Subsurface feeding follows on the emergers as indicated by a porpoising rise form. Surface feeding on the adult insect follows as indicated by splashy rises, observed by open mouths and telltale feeding bubbles.

Now, roosterfish don't feed on a hatch of flatiron herring with a progression similar to trout on flies, but they do follow a progression of observable behavior and aggression going into and out of feeding mode. The stages are different between the small to medium sized fish and the truly big ones. We can loosely categorize roosters into three size classes. The small young of the year are hand size up to about a pound in weight. The locals refer to them as sorillos or skunks. The medium size category runs to the mid to high teens in weight. The big ones, or grandes, take the size class from 20 to 60 plus pounds.

Again we can draw some comparisons in feeding behavior to the relative size of trout. As a general rule, smaller trout feed almost exclusively on insects and tend to feed more hours of the day to fill their stomachs. Small to medium roosterfish also seem to spend more time feeding on small food items and are more susceptible to being fooled by a good presentation. At some point in the growth of trout, they begin to feed on larger food sources such as small fish. These larger fish feed less often and become more cautious outside of the intense feeding cycle, to the point of becoming exclusively night feeders.

Roosterfish follow a similar feeding pattern as they grow and mature. Roosters begin their life feeding on smaller bait fish, the sardina (flatiron herring), being a key food source. As they grow and mature the preference moves towards larger prey species, especially mullet, caballitos, needlefish, ballyhoo, blue runners, greenjacks and eventually ladyfish and small roosterfish. As with the larger trout, the big roosters fill their stomachs faster on the larger food source and spend more time being highly suspicious and seemingly paranoid of fake fish, no matter how good the presentation.

The Tackle

Rods

Small to medium sized roosters can be comfortably handled on eight and nine weight rods. The better-suited rods have a medium fast to a fast action with good casting versus fish fighting characteristics. The nine weight is a good all around beach and boat rod for fishing roosters and the other species that commonly show up with them. Stepping up to the big fish (20 pounds or bigger) a ten weight is the minimum from a casting stand point and a fish fighting perspective. We throw big bulky flies at big fish, so the larger rods tend to be more efficient. The trade off is the number of casts that one can handle in a day, making the 12 weight a lot of rod to cast. We still tend to favor the rods with good casting features over the heavy lifters on big roosters. The roosterfish is as tough as any jack crevalle, and like the big jacks, the pull against the rod is more horizontal than with the tuna where the pull is vertical.

Reels

I prefer direct drive reels with a large arbor. Line capacity for the small to medium fish of 200 yards is adequate. The big fish are best targeted with reels holding 300 yards of 30 lb. Dacron or 50 lb. Spectra. This is especially true for fishing the beach without the ability to chase a fish as you would while fishing from a boat.

Fly Lines

The intermediate sink line is my choice for all size classes of roosters. Integrated sinking lines perform well under windy conditions, as do shooting heads. Floating lines work fine making the presentation to the fish, but give up reel capacity and act as a sail in a cross wind.

Leaders

I use a longer leader for roosters by comparison to other species in the Sea of Cortez, but seldom longer than nine feet. For beach and for boat, a leader with a four foot butt section and three to five feet of class leader is adequate. The tippet breaking strength should match the rod's lifting capability. Big roosters do have small sharp teeth that may abrade a tippet. That said, I seldom put a bite leader on, as break offs due to abrasion have not been a problem. Roosters can be extremely particular about the action of the fly in the water, so I like to keep the leader as clean of knots and connections as possible. A number of talented fly fishermen and guides that have caught lots of big roosters do add a 40 lb. bite leader. Several guides I work with use 30 lb. test for their entire leader. In conversations with my peers, it seems that the use of fluorocarbon is also all over the board. I like the Yo-Zuri hybrid for a number of reasons, but I am not convinced that fluorocarbon is necessary.

The Flies

Size is of considerable importance when targeting roosterfish. The fly must represent the size of the predominate source of food. Fly selection is therefore a continuation of the discussion of size of fish and the food source preference. For the small to medium fish, a good imitation of the sardina covers most situations. Our hottest fly over the past couple of years is the Baja Bucktail Deceiver or BBD in 2/0 to 4/0. The important characteristics that contribute to the success of this fly are its balance when ripped, a head that pushes water and a flowing wing and tail. Color selection is simple, mostly white with pearl flash that extends past the bucktail, with a grey, tan or olive dorsal. The Clouser has been a staple fly for many years and is a good roosterfish fly when they are feeding on sardinas, small needlefish or ballyhoo. I like the Clouser when the sardinas are smaller than three inches, preferring the BBD when the bait is larger. The same color schemes work with the Clouser as with the BBD.

The big roosterfish like big meals, so the fly should imitate the mullet, caballitos, ballyhoo or ladyfish. Mullet patterns with clipped deer hair heads that are sized to match the natural (six to ten inches) on 4/0 to 7/0 hooks are my first choice. Examples are the Baja Muddler and the Beach Rat. I also use a variation of the Rasta. A recent pattern I developed is called the Gym Sock and used it to good success, especially when the bait is bigger than eight inches. Some of the Gym Socks we tie would fit the feet of Shaquille O'Neal. Since its development, the Gym Sock has been highly successful for peacock bass, musky, lake trout, king salmon in the salt, striped bass and billfish.

The Tactics

Earlier in this chapter I introduced the concept of different stages of feeding behavior in roosterfish, as compared to the feeding stages of trout during an insect hatch. Along with that idea I also differentiated between the age classes of roosterfish, again with comparisons to trout. I make the comparisons here in this book, the same as I attempt to do with clients, for the purpose of connecting a known experience from trout fishing, to the new experience of pursuing roosterfish, dorado and the rest. As an aid, I have found that it helps clients focus on a consistent, proven-successful approach for making the right presentation at the right time. Random casts to Roosters while throwing lots of live chum when the fish are not to the proper stage of feeding aggression is akin to the trout fisherman holding to a blind casting a dry fly when the trout are definitely eating nymphs drifting deep in the current. In either case, a few fish may be caught.

In the case of trout fishing, the aesthetics of catching fish on a dry fly is more appealing to some, and a tactic that may be desirable to continue doing. In the case of roosterfish, the odd fish caught out of sequence can lead you astray over the many other days that follow. "Well it worked for me before (meaning maybe once)."

Hitting it right with roosterfish and hooking fish during the height of their frenzy can likewise lead you in the wrong direction. A case in point is the tale of two clients fishing with us on our boat. The first day worked itself into one those incredible days when eventually it all worked. This was after lots of coaching on the merits of hard, fast stripping, keeping the fly on the move, accelerating the fly away from the fish and making the cast right on the teaser.

We started fishing during the initial stage of feeding activity. The clients caught a few fish due to application of proper technique, but not with the frequency to reinforce the tactic from the client's perspective. As the fish moved into the final stages of feeding aggression occasionally any retrieve worked including dead drops and slowing down the movement of the fly in front of pursuing fish. It was a great day for everyone.

I apparently did not emphasize enough how rare such a day was and how important sticking to proper presentation is, under normal conditions. The following four days were more normal in that the fish responded as they usually do with lots of last second refusals; if they followed at all. One client could not get it out of his head what worked the first day was no longer working, and did not apply the technique appropriate to the behavior of the fish. His partner did the right things and continued to catch fish. The difference being, the successful angler made every cast to the teaser, stripped hard and accelerated the retrieve as soon as a roosterfish started to follow. As is normal, he got a lot of refusals, but he stuck with it and had good fishing the next four days.

Not so his friend. The more refusals that he experienced led him to experiment more with his retrieve. The refusals he experienced hardened his resolve to not listen to my coaching. After all, slowing down the retrieve and dead drops worked that first day, didn't they? Over the next four days he caught very few fish. This was an extreme case, but not so far off from what commonly happens after an exceptional day. Most of our clients eventually gain faith in what consistently works and start catching fish again.

Believe me when I say that this fish humbles me to the point of doubting my methods. I went through this same cycle over the past 30 some years in the pursuit of roosterfish. The learning curve was long and steep at first, because I adopted things that worked on the rare occasion and tried to re-apply them to the normal situation. Consistent levels of success followed with gained understanding of the behaviors and I began repeating the things that consistently worked. Believe me, I still go through mental periods of doubt when the roosters are particularly tough to fool and wonder if I really understand much about these magnificent creatures. Roosterfish tactics are a work in progress as we continue to learn more about these incredible game fish. I am sure that I will be writing an update to this chapter in near future.

In the course of our guiding, we have observed a progression of stages in the feeding activity or aggression of roosterfish. In this section I will break down the feeding activity of the fish and the different tactical approaches into four stages as applied to the techniques of chumming, teasing and fishing for the small to medium fish. I will treat the big fish separately. The stages have as much to do with the actual feeding activity of the fish as they do with the chumming techniques used.

In the case of the small to medium sized fish we are usually rigging sardinas as the live teaser as well as throwing them out as free swimming chum. The actual casting and stripping techniques vary less than the chumming and teasing techniques. In reality, the fish and fish-catching techniques have three stages, however there is a super or forth stage that requires some adjustment in the chumming and teasing techniques.

In Chapter Five on presentation, I mention that I would reserve discussion on the stages of feeding behavior to the roosterfish chapter as they are the most difficult of the species we fish to fool. Roosterfish are the poster children for applying recognition of what stage the bite is in and how to adapt techniques accordingly. The second important premise is that what works on roosterfish, works on jacks, dorado, tuna and billfish. In essence this chapter is an extension of Chapter Five using the best example to learn from, namely the rock star of the beaches from La Paz to Peru.

Small to Medium Roosters From the Boat

Continuing with the discussion of the different feeding behaviors between size classes of rooster, I will start with using the stages as a way to describe the behavior and corresponding techniques of the small to medium class fish first, and then go on to the stages as applied to the grandes.

Stage One Fish Behavior, the Curious Non-Feeder

This stage of behavior occurs when the fish are just starting to show some interest in feeding. The fish are essentially responding to their innate curiosity, some hunger and a whole lot of caution. The fish tend to appear from directly behind the teaser, which they will follow for a short period of time. Displays of combing usually don't occur with fish at stage one, but may display a zig zag swimming pattern. They also refuse the tethered live teaser as not being completely natural to them. They will, however, eat free swimming chum thrown into the water, well after they swim away from the boat. This is not the time to throw live chum in the water as the feeding activity takes place well out of casting range. The fish are still sufficiently cautious in regards to taking the fly, especially when there is live natural prey in the water.

Stage One Teasing and Chumming

At this point in the game, the person handling the teaser rod keeps the live teaser in play in front of the fish with little if any attempt to move it away from the approaching fish. Pulling the teaser away from the merely curious fish will surely put it down. Throwing live chum into the water will result in the fish chasing the live swimmers some distance away from the boat before they eat, if they eat at all. I do, however, introduce live chum from time to time to gage the interest of the fish. If there is abundant live chum on board I can, at times, induce the fish into the next level of feeding behavior.

Stage One Tactics

Tactical option one is to keep casting to a tight circle of one yard around the live teaser, make three to four sharp strips, then pick the fly up and place it back on top of the teaser. It is best not to waste time retrieving all the way back to the boat even if the fish follows. At this stage, these cautious fish have already had a good look at the fly, and will tend to refuse at the end of the retrieve. The few susceptible fish are the ones with their noses right behind the live teaser.

Tactical option two is to hold back the cast till the fish is worked up by the teaser. A live teaser left swimming in front of the roosterfish's nose may eventually excite the fish enough to get it to try and eat the teaser. Either way, fish at this stage are very difficult to fool.

A few fish at this stage of feeding will occasionally react instinctively by grabbing a fly that suddenly appears in its target zone. These are the fish you want to concentrate on. Keep in mind that rooster at this stage of the game make up their minds very quickly about the teaser and leave quickly. You don't want your fly elsewhere and miss the short op-portunities as they present themselves. In other words, the more time you have a fly swimming properly in the attack zone in front of the most fish, the greater the chance of a hook up.

There are several other keys to getting a hook up and this applies to all four stages. The first is that the retrieve starts as soon as the fly hits the water. The second is that the retrieve starts fast and accelerates away as soon as the fish shows interest. This can be accomplished with a rod sweep low to the side and away from the fish. We call this a scissor strip, or sweep. If the fish refuses, pick up the line and roll cast back to the fish and follow immediately with another scissor strip. This technique will turn a few stage one fish. A roll cast and scissor strip accomplishes two things: quick repositioning of the fly back to the teaser, and a faster retrieve than you can attain by hand stripping the fly.

Stage Two Behavior, the Finicky Feeder

As the roosterfish's appetite increases, we note changes in behavior. The approach to the teaser is still mostly from behind, but at this stage the rooster will eventually pounce on the teaser, displaying the characteristic zig zag swimming behavior and by raising its comb out of the water.

The stage two fish's reaction to free swimming chum is much like stage one in that they follow it away from the boat before they eat. This is especially true if the chum is thrown any distance from the boat, rather than being dropped right behind the transom.

Stage Two Teasing and Chumming

The person on the teasing rod needs to pay attention to the aggressiveness of the fish in determining when to pull the live teaser away. Pull the teaser too soon and the rooster looses interest altogether. If the person doing the teasing is too slow and misjudges the aggressiveness of the fish, chances are that the fish will grab the live teaser and strip it from the rigging. At this point, I still tend to hold the teaser as close to the fish and move it as little as possible. I like to raise the rod tip and dangle the sardina half way out of the water. This doesn't look natural enough to elicit a strike from the rooster, but it will keep their attention focused long enough for the fisherman to rip a fly across the fish's cone of vision. When timed properly, a hook up may occur.

Beginning at stage two, I like to introduce a few sardinas into the prop wash of the boat where they tend to swim along directly behind the boat for protection. Throwing a few sardinas close to the live teaser sweetens the pot as they like to school up together. Too many live sardinas in the prop wash or with the live teaser tends to focus all the attention on the naturals and distract away from the fly. A rule of thumb is to have fewer live fish in the water than fish coming into the spread. A swarm of four roosters and three available "livies" creates competition between the roosters. Competition for food works in our favor and often results in more hook ups.

Stage Two Tactics

As the fish transition into stage two, I encourage the anglers to cast continuously at the teaser. The window of opportunity is short and the more times that the fly arrives at the teaser the same time as the fish, the higher the percentage of hook ups. The key to getting hook ups rather than follows is by casting to the teaser. Follow the cast up with fast strips or sweeps and keeping the retrieve short.

The fish at this stage don't stay around long and the time spent retrieving the fly all the way to boat will result in missed opportunities at the teaser where the chance of a hook up is highest. One of the hardest concepts for fishermen to grasp is that the fish that follows the fly for any distance at this level of feeding behavior is not likely to eat the fly. It is hard to get fishermen to pull the fly off the nose of a following rooster to reposition the fly back to the teaser. Occasionally it works out that the fish will take, but with a caveat. I like to coach our clients to watch the reaction of the fish when the fly is pulled from the water. If the fish just sort of glides off after the fly disappears from its view, the best choice is to cast right back to the teaser. On the other hand if the fish zig zags in a frantic search for the fly, then an immediate roll cast back to the nose of the fish will sometimes draw a strike.

Stage Three Behavior, the Aggressive Feeder

This is where it really starts to get fun and the number of fish hooked versus follows and refusals increases. Stage three behavior does not occur during every feeding cycle, but we do see this situation fairly often. On most days this is the climax of the feeding cycle and does not last long. A lucky angler may experience a half hour of hot feeding and then the fish are down.

One of the marked differences in fish behavior is that the fish start to appear from not only behind the teaser, but from the sides and even out from under the boat. Their approach to the live teaser is rapid often taking the teaser bait immediately. Combing display occurs quickly along with the zig zag swimming pattern. The fish begin to attack the teaser aggressively along with the sardinas swimming in the prop wash and those swimming alongside the teaser. Fresh "livies" thrown in the vicinity of the boat are attacked quickly and within range of a 40-foot cast.

Stage Three Teasing and Chumming

At this point the person working the teasing rod has to stay on top of things as the roosters will rip the teaser out of its harness quickly. As the fish become aggressive, it becomes more difficult to keep the roosters from eating the bait and the person on the teaser rod has to reel the teaser in quickly as each single or group of roosters approach.

This is where live, free-swimming chum plays a bigger role in gaining multiple hook ups. I begin introducing more chum into the water in order to hold fish that have come to the teaser, especially if the first to arrive have stripped the live teaser and I need to buy some time to re-rig.

Stage Three Tactics

The basic fishing techniques remain the same with continuous casts to the teaser. The teaser is now being pulled quickly away from the fish and towards the boat. This presents a challenge to the fisherman in that the target is closing rapidly to the boat with the resulting cast falling behind the fish. A cast that falls behind the fish seldom results in a hook up. The angler must lead the forward progression of the teaser far enough so that the fly still lands in front of the fish. In the excitement of the moment, this is harder than it sounds and lots of opportunities are blown by over-casting the fish.

Stage Four Behavior, Nirvana

Lucky is the angler who experiences a full-on, stage-four episode. We occasionally create the frenzy with teasers and live chum, but quite often we happen upon schools of roosters crashing schools of bait. The distinction between stage three and stage four is both the increased number of fish that swarm to the teaser, chum or fly and the frenzied aggression they display. Keeping a live teaser in the water becomes very difficult with fish pouncing on it before the person running the teasing rod can pull slack and control the live sardina at the end of the line.

At stage four, the roosters are so intent on feeding that they will hit the fly before they get to the teaser or the free swimming chum. If the fly pattern resembles food and a reasonable retrieve is used, it will be eaten with seeming abandon. Casts that land well beyond the teaser or off to the side of the teaser are grabbed by eager fish. Dead drops and stalled retrieves will also catch some fish.

At this point I put down the teasing rod and simply keep introducing a steady supply of free swimming sardinas into the water directly behind the boat. Again, the rule of thumb is to put fewer "livies" into the water than fish available to keep the edge of competition keen. A hook-less plug used as a teaser can be highly effective with stage four fish and eliminates the use of a live teaser all together.

Teasing Big Roosters from the Boat

Fishing for big roosters from the boat requires a slightly different approach than working the small to medium-sized fish. The key principles are the same, however. The fly must be on target in front of the fish, the fly is stripped fast with acceleration of the retrieve once the fish turns on the fly.

Chumming and teasing techniques for larger roosters are less complicated from the stand point that we usually don't introduce free swimming chum into the water along with the tethered live teaser. We can therefore look at big roosters having three stages of feeding behavior.

Stage One Behavior

As with the smaller fish, the big roosters approach the live chum, usually mullet, with caution and curiosity. The approach is generally from behind without combing or zig zag swimming characteristics. Big roosters will arrive and leave quickly, although a few may return for another look. The actually swimming motion of a large fish at this stage is looser, with a pronounced S-curves in its body and swimming pattern.

Stage One Teasing

When the fish are displaying caution in their approach to the teaser I like to drop the mullet back a good 50 feet or more behind the boat. If the fish follows, I reel the bait slowly towards the boat, dropping the mullet back if the fish leaves. Once we encounter a big rooster that drops off the teaser, we circle the boat back with the hope that he will return. With patience, there are times when a big stage one fish can be excited into eating.

Stage One Tactics

This is the time to hold the fly out of the water until the fish shows some real interest in the mullet. If we are lucky, the fish becomes more interested in the mullet with each pass of the boat. Once the fish starts to get excited and approaches the mullet with intent to eat, make a cast on top of the Mullet and strip it away. Fish that follow the fly for any distance are unlikely to eat the fly, so again, the routine is to pull the fly out of the water and wait for the fish to return to the mullet, where the dance starts again. We have worked on big fish for five to ten minutes before they rev up and get excited enough to eat.

Stage Two Behaviors

These fish will approach from behind as in stage one, but the movement to the bait is more rapid and decisive. Combing behavior followed by zig zagging are telling signs of increased interest on the part of the fish. The body form and swimming pattern is straighter and not the loose flexible style displayed by the stage one fish.

Stage Two Teasing

The person handling the teasing rod must exercise judgment of the fish's behavior and move the bait accordingly. A rate of retrieve slightly faster than the swimming speed of the fish, that smoothly moves the bait towards the boat, is usually the best first approach. Be prepared to sweep the bait away if the fish tries to eat it.

Stage Two Tactics

My experience has been that it is best to hold the cast until the fish show aggression to the teaser. At stage two this takes place quicker than at stage one. Big roosters will often nip at the tail of the mullet before they attack with intent to eat it. Once again, timing is everything, with the best chance coming with delivery of the fly at the moment the fish opens its mouth to eat the live bait.

Stage Three Behaviors

This is the stage we live for when big roosters crash the teaser with abandon. The crushing hit can occur with little or no warning, the fish coming from behind or from the side, the comb rising just before the take.

Stage Three Teasing

Once the fish show the tendency to attack quickly, I shorten up the length of line between the boat and the teaser, keeping it around 30 feet behind the transom. A shallow sandy bottom contrasts well with the dark back of a rooster warning the person on the teasing rod, giving them time to pull the bait away from the fish. Glare on the water or fish encountered over dark bottom are hard to detect until they hit the bait. The only option here is to gently, but firmly pull the bait from the fish's mouth with the hope that the mullet will come free and still be attached to the leader. Repeated, vicious strikes often occur resulting in a completely scaled mullet. With luck, the rooster takes the fly instead.

Stage Three Tactics

With aggressive fish, I like to alternate between continuous casts to the teaser and holding the fly out until the attack. All day casting with a 12 weight and a bulky fly is fatiguing and distracting to your focus. The objective is to deliver the fly at the point of attack, or if the bait is swallowed, when it comes free again. The good news is that you will usually have multiple shots at fish that are worked up and aggressive. All the other principles apply: fly placement on the nose, starting the strip in air, rapid stripping followed by a sweep as soon as the fish turns on the fly.

Beach Fishing for Roosterfish

For many, the ultimate challenge is fishing for roosterfish from the beach, and there is no place better than the East Cape region of the Baja. This is not a game of numbers most of the time, although I have experienced some highly productive days. The beach requires patience, physical stamina and keen observation. The windows of opportunity are exceedingly small and require you to always be ready with tackle and presence of mind.

As in the earlier part of this chapter, I will endeavor to separate the tactical approach to roosterfish by size class.

Beach Fishing for Small to Medium Roosters

The smaller fish come and go all season, depending on food availability and provide great sport when present. The small to medium-sized roosters are fairly consistent in where they are found, that being where ever the sardinas, ballyhoo or needlefish are pushed against the shore.

Flies for Small to Medium Roosters

My choice of flies starts with sardina imitations, sized to match the prevalent bait I observe swimming along the shore line. Small needlefish and ballyhoo imitations are also good choices for the beach. I like Clouser-type patterns for the beach as they give me the option to allow the fly to sink quickly if the need arises, such as trying to fish the underside of a bait ball. I tie them long and skinny for the ballyhoo and full dressed for the sardinas. Other patterns that are effective are the BBD, Rasta, Sea Habits, various sardina patterns and crease flies. Poppers can be effective at times, especially during low light and when cast next to a surface plug teaser.

Tackle for Small to Medium Roosters

I like rods in the nine to ten weight range, and a good saltwater reel loaded with an intermediate sink line. When the troughs are deep, the current strong or the wind is blowing, I prefer a sink tip or full sink line. Either choice of lines will work most of the time. I build my leaders with a ferruled butt and 15 to 20 lb. class tippets with no bite leader and to a length of seven to nine feet.

Tactics for Small to Medium Roosters

To catch roosters from the beach, I first look for actual feeding activity of fish, followed in choice by looking for pods of bait. Blind casting to feeding fish or visible pods of bait will often produce smaller roosters. Fast single-hand or double-hand strips along with scissor strips at the end of the retrieve work to receptive fish. A bonus here is that other species follow the same schools of bait fish and can add variety to the day. Other available species typically include varieties of jacks, ladyfish, Mexican look downs, pompano, croakers, bonefish, needlefish and various species of pargo. They all take the same flies and respond to the retrieves used for the roosters.

When the presence of bait and feeding activity is not visible, I concentrate my search in areas of fishy beach structure and blind cast to those spots. I like to cruise the beach at low tide and high sun to determine the best structure. This combination of light and low water reveals the structure and clues as where to look. Wind patterns change the structure of the sandy beaches on a weekly basis, so constant scouting and adjustment is needed.

Two of the key bottom features I look for are troughs and bars. A change in water color exposes both. With good light and a low tide, the bars stand out as a greenish tan color, while the deeper troughs are more blue green in color. I start by looking down the shore line and picking out the minor sandy points or finger bars that run out into the deeper water. These projections are usually subtle in appearance and can even disappear from view when you come up on top of them.

A trick I use, is to pick out an object on the shore line adjacent to the point, and walk or drive directly to that spot. Once I am on top of the point, I look for a trough of deeper water that usually forms on both sides of the point itself. Water current due to tidal change flows across the shallow finger bars and cuts a trough on either side of the bar, much like a riffle in a river forms a hole or deeper run on the down-current side. Bait fish gravitate to these troughs for shelter and to feed on plant life that collects there due to current movement, and the predators follow. Since there is usually a trough on either side of the bar, I concentrate on the water that is down current from that point. In other words, if the tide is falling I fish the down current side of the point. I fish the opposite side of the point on an incoming tide.

Another feature that I look for is an offshore bar that forms parallel to the beach. These bars usually form along beaches with prominent points and coves. The bars form as close as 40 to 50 feet from the beach and tie into the finger points. These are natural funnels that push cruising roosterfish and jacks close to shore. Big fish follow these systems of troughs and bars in their search for mullet, small ladyfish and other target prey.

Line Management in the Surf

One of the challenges of fishing the surf is what to do about the wave wash and all that loose line stripped off the reel and ready to cast. The aggravation factor begins to peg out, as the wind and wave action increases. One option is to use a stripping basket. Stripper fishermen are used to using them and they do a good job handling loose line. Baskets are seen along the beaches of the Baja attached to the hips of some very successful rooster fishermen. I personally find them awkward to strip line into at the speed necessary to catch fish, though I do like them for line storage while on the move from one prime spot to the other.

So how do I deal with the sometimes vexing wave wash without using a basket to strip into? For one thing, in many cases you don't have to wade into the water to shorten casting distance to the fish. When they are feeding, the action tends to be very close to the beach. When I do wade in, I find the sweet spot in the waves where the sand is never exposed by the retreating wash, nor so deep that I am fighting the curling wave. Look for a shallow trough that forms where the small wind waves of the Cortez lap the shoreline. There is less swirl and back wash there, and in most cases the water is only knee deep. This is also a good position to stand and make a cast parallel to the shore line. This same wave trough is also the place that the predators like to trap the bait fish and commit feeding mayhem.

This pronounced wave trough is commonly formed in the Sea of Cortez with its very gentle to non-existent surf. The beaches of the Pacific side of the Baja and Central America can present much larger and rougher surf conditions that preclude finding, much less standing along the wave trough. In big surf, I do resort to a stripping basket for more than line storage.

Another wading trick is to figure the slight angle that waves usually hit the shore line and side-step along into the wash. Your fly line will tend to flow behind you and not around your ankles. Standing for too long in one spot is a sure invitation for entanglement. Along with this tip, step out of the water if you are not casting and keep your line on dry sand. Standing in the back wash while changing flies, adding tippet to your leader or just gazing across this magnificent land and seascape will get you thoroughly wrapped up in a way not given to a quick presentation to a fast approaching fish. And, they will approach in a hurry, often when you are least prepared. To be successful keep your focus, watch the trough line constantly and have your line ready.

Once the glare is off the water from a higher sun angle and sight fishing becomes possible, the game changes. I stop blind-casting into the troughs for smaller fish and spend more time watching for the big roosters to cross a bar into a trough. The object of the game then, is to position in front of the cruising fish and wait for them to come into casting range, the supreme challenge of beach fishing on the Baja.

Beach Fishing for Big Roosters

In recent years there has been a huge surge of interest in fly fishing for big roosters from the beach. Magazine articles and the video, *Running down the Man* have made popular this highly specialized and challenging sport. Without a doubt, the taking of a 20-plus pound roosterfish from the beach is one the highest accomplishments attainable on a fly rod.

So many things conspire against our attempts to catch them, the first of which is the temperament of the fish itself. They can be aggressive at times to respond to the fly, but most often are extremely wary of anything that is not live bait. Add to this the difficulty of making a presentation from the beach, the closing speed of the target, the effect of wind on casting, grinding heat and water conditions. Keep in mind that all of these conditions are often amplified by having to run in order to get into position to make a presentation.

When I began my pursuit of this remarkable game fish some thirty years ago, they were considered impossible to catch in any form other than with live bait. And even then were considered difficult. Well, they are still difficult and a true angling trophy regardless of the tackle, but they are not impossible. In this section I will share what we have learned so far about fishing roosters from the beach. This is definitely a collected body of knowledge gained over the years by friends, clients, guides and partners of the Baja Flyfishing Co.

Previously, I have broken the feeding behavior and tactical approaches to that feeding behavior into various stages. In the case of big roosters from the beach, however, I haven't found an appropriate application for several reasons. The first reason is that if the big guys are prowling the beach, they are usually in search of food and are ready to eat if the presentation is right. This is not to say that we don't encounter groups, or singles traveling through on some other business, such as seeking mating opportunities. The second reason is that on the beach, the tactical approach is more limited as compared to the boat, both by being land bound and lacking the ability to tease with live bait.

Big roosters can show any time from March on with the peak of activity along the beach occurring in late May into late June. By about the third week in June we start to see a decline in numbers close to shore and begin observe a daisy chain swimming pattern that has been interpreted as a spawn or pre-spawn activity. I do not pretend to know much about the biology of these fish and research is very scant on their life cycles, spawning activities, longevity or migration. So we are left to speculate on the behavior that we observe and one of the things that we have noted is that when the roosters are daisy-chaining, they are not feeding. We see much of the same behavior with the jack crevalles earlier in the spring.

Beach Tactics for Big Roosters

The pursuit of big roosters on the beach has turned into a thirty year obsession for me, a passion that is as strong now as it has ever been. Fishing for a true grande has all the elements of hunting where spotting, stalking and at times running the quarry down is involved. Very few large roosters are caught from the beach by blind casting. This is a visual game that requires, spotting, planning and positioning before the presentation can be made. Like hunting, the angler, in many cases, has but one shot at the fish.

The first step is to figure out where and when to look for the big fish that are cruising the beaches. That process begins with finding their food source. Mullet are a main staple in the diet of big roosters, so this is where I initiate my search. Mullet are small-particle vegetarians, and as such are dependent on wind, tide and structure to gather and concentrate their food source. I begin my search by looking for shoreline structures that capture the food source, such as small bays, coves and back eddies formed by points. Deep troughs formed on the down-current side of sand bars are also collection points, much as the deep runs below a riffle are feeding posts for trout. These locations, at least in general, can hold fish for as long as the bait is present and the structure stays intact. Bars and troughs change through the fishing season as the winds transition from the winter Northerlies to the summer South Easterlies. Keep in mind that a single wind event can drastically change the shore line structure as the sands are pushed and rocks are covered and uncovered.

When to present is more dynamic, changing hourly with wind and tide. Tidal movement varies by location. The Sea of Cortez, in the regions where roosterfish are common, does not experience as great a tidal fluctuation as parts of Central America. In and around Gulfito, Costa Rica, the tidal change is dramatic with strong associated currents and the feeding behavior distinctly follows the strongest tidal flows. Flood and falling tides create the strongest currents and concentrate bait fish behind any structure that slows the current such as bars, rock structure and points. The Sea of Cortez has less dramatic tidal changes and interacts more with wind conditions. The large roosterfish congregate along the East Cape about the time that the South Easterly winds start to blow in the afternoons in late May and June. This afternoon, on-shore wind pushes the food source and concentrates it along shoreline structure. Find where the wind pushes directly into troughs and coves and you are likely to find concentrations of mullet. Tidal movement that occurs with the time that the South Easterly winds pick up is prime time for hunting big roosterfish. The broad, magic time period for big roosterfish on the beach is between 11:00 am and 4:00 pm. Tidal movement during this time period will further focus when peak feeding will occur.

The when and where being established, the rest falls on persistent vigilance. While the large fish are easy to spot in contrast to the sandy bottom, they approach and pass very quickly, leaving you a small window of opportunity to make a presentation. Hail Mary shots at ninety-degree angles to the target, or at departing fish seldom do more than spook or at minimum alert fish to your presence. They may even turn and follow the fly out of curiosity, but their intuitive sense will tell them that the object of their interest is not acting like food should act.

I advocate letting a poor shot opportunity to pass you by with the hope that the same fish will work its patrol circuit and return past your position. Quite often big roosters run a patterned patrol through prime hunting areas and will return. Be ready for them with line stripped into a basket or onto the sand to the expected casting length. There is not time for a lot of false casting to build a lengthy cast. Stripping baskets are their most useful as a storage place for line while waiting for fish to appear, or to hold line while you dash ahead to gain a good casting position. As stated earlier, I personally don't strip line back into a stripping basket after my first cast to the fish, as I find the basket inhibits my fastest possible stripping speed. This is a personal skill-related thing for me, as I know several very good roosterfish anglers that expertly use a basket.

My experience as a guide and fisherman has taught me how important speed and consistency are in the strip cadence on these fish under normal conditions. Bear in mind, that in an all-out bust, the fish are less selective and less than ideal presentation will work. Here again, I differentiate between things I do causing a fish to follow and resulting in a refusal and what I do to get a fish to eat. I look at stripping baskets like I do the double-hand strip, if you have the skill to properly use it, do it. If the process is at all awkward to the point of disrupting the flow of the strip, then go with what works best for you to obtain the optimal speed and consistency of stripping.

Back to sight fishing big roosters on the beach. Once the fish is spotted, move into position to make the cast. The best situation is when the cast can be made on the nose of the fish and then pulled directly away from it and in the direction of the travel pattern of the fish. Casts that result in the fly crossing the nose of the fish or coming up from behind should be avoided at all costs. It is better to move ahead of the fish in order to cast back to it or let it go by and wait for it to return than to spook it with a Hail Mary cast.

I begin my strip while the fly is still in the air so that the fish never sees the fly settling in the water, or has the opportunity to scrutinize it closely. I strip as fast as my hands will work and begin a sweep with the rod to accelerate the movement of the fly as soon as the fish turns on it. I don't want to encourage the fish to follow the fly for any distance, as that most often results in a high speed refusal. I take the game to the fish and force them to make a quick decision about whether to eat or not. Backing up while stripping is an alternative that works well to accelerate the fly and to reduce the pauses caused by a single hand retrieve.

When cruising fish are not visible along the shoreline, I break out the spin rod and throw hook-less teasers with the hope of pulling a fish. When the fish are responsive, this can be an effective technique. This tactic requires team work and timing between the person doing the teasing, and the person casting the fly. The fly should land three to six feet in front of the approaching teaser and stripped in the same line of movement as the teaser. Poppers work their best magic when fished in conjunction with a teaser. The chapter on presentation covers lures and techniques for beach teasing.

Photograph by Brian O'Keefe

Photograph by Eric Kummerfeldt

8

Jacks:

Cousin to the Roosterfish from a Family of Bruisers

I remember a time when the jack crevalle was considered a trash fish and was generally shunned by serious anglers. I could never understand that sentiment, as they typify the jack species as aggressive feeders and extremely tough fighters. You got to love a fish that slams poppers, burns into the backing, and then fights you every inch of the way.

My love affair with jacks started on my very first trip to the Baja over thirty years ago. The fish was a four or five pound crevalle that kicked butt on a seven weight Fenwick glass rod. The image of that fish peeling out of the school to inhale my fly is burned into my brain, and I seek every opportunity to relive that wonderful memory.

The crevalles are a member of the jack species which also includes the yellowtail, amberjack, blackjack, big eye jack, greenjack, rainbow runner, horseeye jack, roosterfish, trevalles, pampano and many others, all of which are found in the Sea of Cortez and the Pacific beyond. For me, the crevalle is king of the jacks as far as the fly rod goes, so much of my discussion in this chapter focuses on them with references to the other cousins.

The Tackle

The same rods, reels, leaders and flies that we use for roosters apply to the jacks. The smaller members of the species are perfect eight or nine weight fish. A big crevalle is a respectable opponent, and worthy of a twelve weight rod and that is what I grab when I am certain that the bigger fish are around. If you are in doubt as to what will show up next in size and don't want to throw a big rod all day, the ten weight is a good compromise.

Lines

An intermediate line will handle almost all jack fishing situations. My second choice would be an integrated sink tip line, followed by a floating line, especially if I plan on throwing a lot of poppers.

Leaders

A seven- to nine-foot leader that matches the rod size and fish works well. I don't tend to put a bite leader on for jacks. In other words, the same leader set ups for roosters are ideal for jacks.

The Tactics

The tactics that work for roosters work well for jacks. The crevalles and their cousins respond well to teasing, both with live bait and hook-less plugs. Jacks are often found feeding with roosters along the beaches and occasionally together over deeper reefs. I use the same stripping techniques when the fish are slamming live bait or following a teaser. The big difference between the jacks and roosters is that jacks feed on dead bait and will hit a fly on the dead drop. There are times when the dead drop will out fish a fast retrieve. Switching back and forth is a sound approach to getting hooked up. Once the fish are up and feeding, I throw live chum as well as a few dead ones and watch for the reaction. If the jacks stay on the swimmers, then the retrieve should be fast and on the surface. If they pounce on the dead sardinas then I switch to the dead drop. The Clouser is a good jack pattern as it fishes both the fast strip and dead drop well.

Jacks can be found working baitfish along the sandy beach at first day light. As the sun comes up they tend to move off and hold around rock structure until the need to feed again pushes them in search of sardina, mullet or ballyhoo. Quite often jacks will reappear along the beaches during the mid-morning and then again in the late afternoon.

Some of the largest jacks we have encountered in the Sea of Cortez were found in large schools swimming several miles offshore. With dark backs and silvery sides, these offshore hunters contrast with the buff colored fish encountered in the shallows beach waters. Quite often these offshore schools are swimming on the surface in tight formation and are extremely spooky to an approaching boat. A good Captain will quietly position the boat ahead of the moving school. I like to throw a large pencil popper ahead of the school and wait to begin the retrieve until the fish close within ten feet. The reaction is either an explosion of fish trying to inhale the lure, or the whole school fleeing to the depths. Live bait thrown in front of the schools can bring the same response. If the fish are in the mood to feed, the action can be frantic. Fast retrieves placed in front of the hookless lure or close to a free-swimming sardina have the best chance of bringing on a savage strike. I like sardina patterns with lots of flash in these situations.

A situation often encountered in the spring, is large schools of crevalles swimming in tight daisy chains. The Captains refer to these fish as "jurel prieto," or tight jacks. They seem to have mating on their minds and are very spooky fish to approach. Again, quiet positioning of the boat is necessary to avoid blowing the school apart. In many cases however, the school quickly reforms and goes on its daisy-chaining way. By being persistent, we have on occasion found a fish with more than sex on its mind. A Clouser fished on the dead drop has proven to be occasionally effective in this situation. More often than not, fish in the daisy chain have other things to do than entertain fly anglers.

Photograph by Eric Kummerfeldt

9

Dorado:
Everybody's Favorite

The dorado is a very popular fish in the Sea of Cortez as it is in other parts of the world. In other waters it is known as the dolphin fish or mahi mahi. Dorado are aggressive feeders, taking flies and poppers readily, when in the mood to eat. They are strong fighters on fly tackle, usually displaying numerous jumps followed by strong runs. These fish are no quitters either and can press the game at the boat by turning their broad sides against the pull of the rod. Typical school-size fish run 8 to 12 pounds and may number into the hundreds of fish. The bulls (mature males), run large on the East Cape and Central America often weighing over 70 lbs. Fish over 50 lbs. have been caught often by fly fishermen fishing out of these waters.

The Tackle

Rods

A nine weight is the minimum size stick for school-size dorado, especially for casting small flies on calm days. The ten-through twelve-weight rods are a better choice while fishing offshore, especially when the larger bulls and other species may be encountered. My recommendation is go with the 12 weight or a Temple Fork Blue Water Light. A light rod and big fish is a tough combination for both fisher and fish, especially if you plan to release the dorado.

Reels

A good-quality, salt-water reel that holds 300 yards of 30 lb. backing is recommended. Large arbor reels with a direct drive is my choice.

Fly Lines

Use full-length intermediate, full-length integrated sinking lines, or shooting heads and floating lines.

Leaders

Use a six to seven foot leader with loop-to-loop connections. A bite tippet is not necessary for dorado, but I often incorporate a 50 or 60 lb. soft bite tippet to facilitate handling fish we intend to release. As with the other species, we match the class tippet to the rod weight with 10 to 12 lb. test on the 8 and 9 weight rods, 12 to 16 lb. test on the 10 and 11 weight rods and 20 lb. test on the 12 weight and heavier rods.

Flies

Matching the hatch to sardinas, I recommend Mosca Magic in 3/0, Clouser minnow in 1/0 to 3/0, BBDs in 3/0, Sea Habit in 1/0 to 3/0, Crease fly in 4/0 as well as Deceivers, Sal Mar Mac, and assorted poppers. My favorite colors include: pearl flashabou with a contrasting blue or dark olive crystal flash topping, white body of natural or artificial hair mixed with crystal flash followed by an olive, tan, blue, grey or chartreuse topping, purple for dark days, and red and white for your basic attractor fly. The boat captains swear by red and white for dorado whether you are fishing with flies or lures on conventional gear.

Squid are an important food source in the Sea of Cortez for all off-shore species, including dorado, and a selection of squid flies should be included with your gear. Squid have the ability to change color based on water clarity or state of excitement. When undisturbed, their coloration varies from a dirty whitish tan to dark mottled brown. Squid often display blotches of red on white to a solid deep purple color when they are being preyed upon. That may explain the red and white color preference.

The Tactics

A number of approaches work at different times and under different circumstances. A favorite method is to look for floating debris such as sargasso weed, dead whales, and shark buoys etc. The boat approaches from up wind and drifts to about 60 feet from the floating object. Usually a few live sardinas are thrown close to the debris to see if any fish are present. If swirls occur, the angler throws a fly and gets ready to set the hook. This is a good time to try surface poppers. If this doesn't work, or if the actions slow down on the poppers, then switch to a sardina imitation. We have spent several hours around a single shark buoy casting to fish suspended below the float.

A number of years ago we were running out to the shark buoys in search of dorado when the Captain spotted a floating object some distance off. As we closed in, the Captain and deckhand started shouting "mota (marijuana)!" Sure enough, wrapped in black plastic, floating serenely on the waters of the Cortez was a pirate's booty of dope. Nervously, I started looking for a cigarette boat zooming in, guns drawn or the Federales looking to make a bust. Either scenario in my wild imagination ended badly. In as calm a voice as I could muster, I asked the Captain what his plan was. He replied, "We will bring it aboard and cut the shit up and throw it back in the ocean. " As it turns out, the sport Captains place the dope smugglers right alongside the long liners and tuna purse seiners as a direct threat to their livelihood. Feeling somewhat assured that we weren't headed for a movie plot for being in the wrong place at the wrong time, I asked: "Are we going to check it for fish first?" The Captain looked at me like I was daft and replied, "Como no," meaning "of course." Four dorado later, we hauled the bale aboard, cut the kilos open and dumped untold thousands of dollars in dope overboard. The deckhand was careful to wash every seed and stem through the bilge and into the glittering placid waters of the Cortez.

Another method that pays off well, is to look for feeding fish. This is no brainer fishing excitement at its best. The presence of birds circling and diving is an indicator of the presence of feeding dorado. On calm flat days, dorado can be located by the V-wake created by their heads as they cruise along just under the surface. In any of these cases, the boat should be positioned in front of the movement of the fish, and live chum thrown overboard to entice the dorado closer the boat. Hookless teasers can also be effective in bringing fish closer to the boat. Once the fish are lured into range, flies are thrown close to the live chum slaughter and the fun begins. Some feeding frenzies in the Sea of Cortez are monstrous with many species feeding in the same area. We have been surprised by unexpected hook ups with sailfish and wahoo in the middle of large feeding frenzies. Yellowfin tuna and skipjack are probably the most frequently found fish along with the dorado under these situations.

Dorado are known to be open water feeders, moving great distances in the effort to find enough food to maintain their very high metabolisms. We have also found that dorado, like tuna, will stay around under water structures such as humps, ridges and canyons. When the fish are concentrated in these areas, it pays to shut the boat down over the structure and chum with bloody chunks of skipjack or bonito. It is prudent to hang the carcasses of the fish over the side to create a good blood trail. If you have a bunch of dead sardinas in the bait tank, this is the time and place to use them. I like to wait about five to ten minutes after throwing the first chunks of skipjack before chumming with a handful of dead sardinas. Once the dead sardinas disappear from sight into the depths, I repeat the process. We have pulled in lots of schools of dorado in this fashion along with the occasional yellowfin, wahoo, skipjack, rainbow runner, jack crevalle, pargo and triggerfish.

The fourth, and often the most common way to locate schools of dorado, is to troll flies in order to find the schools. The idea of trolling the fly may not appeal to a lot of fly fishermen, especially trout fishermen new to the saltwater game. The ocean is a huge bucket, as my partner John is wont to say, and the fish can be scattered over a great expanse of water. When fish can't be found over structures or under floating debris, trolling helps to locate schools.

Is the act of trolling a fly with a motorized craft truly fly fishing? It certainly isn't by IGFA standards when it comes to registering a record catch. I am not a card-carrying member of the fly fishing morals committee, and don't intend to pass judgment on what you call trolling the fly, or the ethics of the act. The more important question is does it lead to fly fishing fun and excitement. To that I say yes! I approach the idea of trolling the fly much like sitting in the boat, staked out for hours on end in the hope of casting a fly to tarpon. Lots of time can pass in either situation with all the excitement of watching jerky dry, 'til you find fish. In both cases, I find appeal in the anticipation of encountering fish that I can cast the fly to. I might suggest that the act of trolling the fly is at least a part of the fly fishing process and leave the definition of fly fishing at that. The question that I often hear in regards to trolling the fly is why use fly tackle at all for the process of locating fish? Again this is a question of choice. As a guide, I approach a fish caught on fly tackle as a learning experience for our clients.

Fish caught on the troll allows the angler new to the power of saltwater fish, the opportunity to concentrate on playing the fish without the complexities of first casting, retrieving the fly and setting the hook. Once the school is located, the emphasis can shift to casting, proper presentation and setting the hook. With the experience of playing a strong saltwater species behind us, there is less chance that the angler will break the fish off within seconds of making their first cast. Besides, any saltwater fish hooked by any means on fly tackle is an absolute hoot. The degree of fun that we have is only limited by our biases.

Once a Dorado hits the trolled fly, the fun begins. The object here is to first locate the school, then get them close to the boat where the fly fisher can sight cast to feeding fish. Troll hooked fish don't always show right away at the boat as the fish attempts to follow the rest of the school. In the past few seasons I have taken to throwing a hook-less teaser immediately back to where the hook up occurs. I keep a spin rod handy at the transom for this purpose with a top water plug that casts a long distance. This tactic has brought more fish to the boat. They come quicker and they are hot when they get there.

My favorite ranger lures are well chewed up by dorado teeth. Until I started throwing the lure, we would do a little prospecting with some live sardinas to see if any fish are nearby. If the school was moving away from the boat, this offering went unnoticed. Another enticement is to throw a tethered skipjack carcass over the side, but otherwise we would patiently watch to see if the hooked fish has brought any friends closer to the boat. The teaser lure ensures more fish coming to the boat and expedites the process. When other fish are spotted around the hooked fish, sardinas are again thrown into the water and the frenzy begins. Quite often we will hand the rod to the deckhand to keep the hooked fish in the water close to the boat until more fish are hooked, or the live chum has worked its charm. This gives the angler the chance to pick up another rod rigged to cast to the fish. The live chum and hooked fish can keep large schools of dorado close to the boat for up to an hour on some days.

Why do dorado follow a hooked fish? I don't think it has to do with a romantic connection as some advocate, but rather a feeding response. We have observed many fish regurgitate their stomach contents after being hooked and a host of others rush in to clean up the goodies. We went so far as to cast flesh flies from our Alaskan fly boxes to great success. We have also observed other fish chasing the hooked fish in the attempt to pull the fly from the hooked fish's mouth. One of the reasons I think the Mosca Magic is so effective as a trolling fly is the visibility factor of the fly in the fish's mouth bringing the school closer to the boat. Tube flies have an advantage in that the fly often rides up the leader and is visible to the rest of the school.

The first arrivals to the boat are usually eager feeders and readily take the fly. These fish can be considered stage three feeders and most presentations will work on these fish. I have often witnessed fish taking flies dangling over the side of the boat, while the angler was stripping out line in preparation of the cast. It gets steadily tougher after the first few fish are hooked up. With the large number of fish in any school, it follows that within the school will be stage-one to stage-three feeders. Occasionally, the whole school can be a tough sell getting them to take a fly.

Stage One Behavior and Tactics

The key to identifying feeding responses of stage-one fish are those that swim aimlessly through the school in a large lazy S pattern, paying little attention to the chum. They may follow the chum a ways away from the boat before they eat. These fish are seldom lit up, showing their normal yellow/green colorations. Ignore these fish as they are extremely difficult to get on the fly and concentrate your effort on the stage-two and stage-three fish.

Stage Two Behavior and Tactics

Stage-two fish are easy to pick out of the school. These fish swim with more purpose through the school, with quick, nervous movement. Dorado in stage two display partial to complete electric blue color change. Their reaction to the free swimming chum is more aggressive than in stage one and they tend to feed close to the boat. However, their response over all to the fly is still cautious with follows and no takes. Some dorado may rush the fly ending in a last second refusal, reminiscent of roosterfish.

Several keys are important to getting hook ups with stage-two fish. The timing of throwing bait into the water and presenting the fly to the fish at the same time is critical. The direct method of presentation is used here with the fly thrown close to and in front of the feeding fish and moved as quickly as you can strip the fly away. This often means a fast single-handed retrieve that transitions into a scissor strip. The roll cast and sweep method can be deadly on stage-two fish, providing the speed they expect to see in the natural swimming bait. As stated above in the discussion of stage-one fish, focus the attention on the fish feeding close to the boat that are lit up and ready to pounce on live sardinas. Fish that are lit up are excited fish and appear neon blue in color. Bluefish with dark bars are starting to lose interest and tend to be less aggressive.

A variation to this is to throw the fly into the water followed by the deck hand throwing bait near to the fly. Wait 'til a fish starts to feed, then quickly retrieve the fly past the feeding fish. In other words, this is an intercept presentation. This is not my first choice as it gives the fish a chance to become habituated to the presence of a non-food item. Years of observing feeding behavior has taught us that schools of fish are quick to learn that the fly is a fake and will avoid it. The intercept approach has its advantages with anglers who have weak casting skills, under high wind conditions or on a crowded boat that limits the ability to make a good cast.

In most cases, the fish will be fairly selective to size and color once live chum is thrown into the water. As stated above, fish can also get stale after seeing the same pattern over and over. This is a good time to try poppers or a different pattern. Sometimes the bigger bull dorado hang below the school-sized fish. This is the time to put on the large attractor pattern and let it sink below the school-sized fish. The larger fish are often looking for an easy meal and will occasionally take the fly on the drop, probably thinking they are gathering in a crippled baitfish. If the fly isn't taken on the drop, try a jigging motion, followed by steady, long strip to the surface. This method is also very effective on tuna, wahoo, jacks and skipjacks.

Stage Three Behavior and Tactics

These fish are very easy to recognize. Their movement is rapid and direct to where ever the food source is, often over-taking the less aggressive fish in taking the chum or the fly. Stage-three dorado are lit up neon blue that fairly vibrates in intensity. Fishing to these fish is easy as they will take most speeds of retrieve. The caution here is that once the stage-three fish have been caught, you can be seduced into fishing the rest of the school in the same way. You will have a hard time of it if you continue stripping with a slow, even cadence. I am of the firm belief that you should fish to all the fish as if they are stage-two fish, because stage-one fish are mostly uncatchable. The keys are the same as with rooster-fish in that a fly placed on the nose, stripped fast then swept away will draw the most strikes. In the case of dorado, the schools are often large enough that you can pick your best opportunity fish out of the group.

A variation on the trolling method to locate fish, is to snap a live bait on a swivel and slow troll much as we do for roosterfish. This has become an increasingly popular and effective method with our clients and one we employ when fish are more concentrated in known fishy areas. The disadvantage of a two knot versus a six knot trolling speed is the amount of water that you can cover. Several locations such as the Pulmo sea mounts, Gordos, the canyons in front of Los Barriles and la Ribera come to mind. The other time we switch to this method is when we get a single fish strike, but no following school. After landing the fish, we circle the area with the live bait teaser in the hope that the school is somewhere around. To compensate for the slower trolling speed and less water covered, we will often add a herring dodger, flashers or some variety of daisy chain teasers close behind the boat. I have watched the heads of dorado knifing through the water from a hundred yards out to investigate the teasers we were pulling behind the boat. Occasionally tossing a surface plug sans hooks helps to relocate the school.

Photograph by the author

10

Yellowfin Tuna:
Can You Say Sashimi?

For sheer pulling power, the tuna is probably tougher than any other fish commonly caught on a fly rod in the tropical Pacific. The fight starts with an fast first sprint that goes well into the backing. Following the first run, tuna tend to go deep and circle under the boat. The fight can last longer for a 20 lb. class fish than most sailfish, especially if you are not aggressive in pressing the fight. Yellowfin, like dorado, are found worldwide in semi-tropical to tropical waters.

The Tactics

Tactics for tuna take two main forms: chumming fish up from deep structure, and finding fish feeding with the porpoise.

Tuna on Structures

Tuna can be very structure oriented at times. Underwater ridges, humps, canyon walls, banks and sea mounts that rise out of deeper water form a conduit that concentrates the movement of plankton to the surface. Ocean currents follow these under sea features, carrying the food source to the surface and to the waiting baitfish that in turn feed the tuna.

The process begins with the Captain maneuvering the boat over the structure. Once in place, the deckhand tosses live or dead chum over board. If the tuna are around, they will begin to boil on the live bait. When the action is hot, the tuna can be caught with fast retrieves just under the surface. There are times when poppers will pull fish and bring sav-

age strikes. Hookless top water teasers are effective in bringing tuna closer to the boat. Chugger-type lures that make
a lot of disturbance usually pull more fish than the pencil
poppers and torpedo-shaped bass lures. In the early years
of my blue water experience, a rubber ball on a spin rod was
used to pull tuna or bonito up to the surface. This inexpen-
sive teaser was often referred to as a Bonito Bouncer, and
although I haven't rigged one in many years, I am sure that
they are still as effective as when we threw them along the
kelp beds for bonito and bass.

Tuna hitting a surface retrieve would be, in the Roosterfish vernacular, a stage-three fish. However, we encounter far more stage-two fish that will take the free swimming
chum swimming on the surface, but ignore the fly. In this
instance a sink and rip presentation can be very effective.
Sinking lines in the 400 to 700 grain class come into play
along with a weighted fly such as the Clouser. To gain maximum depth, the fly is cast down-drift of the boat. The drift
of the boat can be determined by either wind or current,
whichever is stronger. A cast up-drift will plane the line up
in the water column due to the pull of the drifting boat. The
object then is to set the boat up at a 90 degree angle to the
drift and place an angler in the front and back.

The cast is made down-drift and to an angle of between
20 to 45 degrees away from the boat. As the boat drifts along,
it allows the line to sink at its maximum rate, in a way mend-
ing the line deeper. The fly is cast at an angle away from the
boat so that the boat doesn't drift over the top of the line.
A good cast will place the line in such a way that the boat
drifts past the line at the same time that the line is straight
down and by that point as deep as sixty or more feet.

Additional depth can be obtained by stripping line off the
reel immediately after the cast and feeding it out as the boat
drifts up on it. Once the line is at maximum depth, usually
when the boat passes the line at the stern or bow, several
techniques can be employed. By lifting and dropping the
rod tip, the fly can be jigged while remaining at the deepest

point of the drift. The amount of time depends on the speed of the drifting boat and at some point the drift will tend to start planing the line toward the surface. At this point, a fast single- or double-hand retrieve to the surface may bring a strike.

Another approach is to allow the fly to sink to its maximum depth and as the boat starts to pass the line, then stick the rod tip into the water, lift and strip at the same time. This is reminiscent of the action taken by conventional gear fishermen in the use of iron or butterfly jigs. In the ripping process, be aware of where the rod tip is. If the strike occurs when the rod is too high over head, the force of the strike can break the tip of the rod. Be ready for the strike and give with the rod. If you maintain tension on the line, the fish will set itself as it usually takes going down and away at a high rate of speed.

A strike may occur at several points in the presentation. Tuna will take the fly on the dead drop, usually at about 12 foot depth or about the point that the fly disappears from sight. Most takes are on the jig or rip, so be aware of the rod angle and be ready to give to the strike. Tuna will also take the fly while being retrieved to the surface.

Tuna Working with Porpoise

The other method involves locating feeding tuna associated with large schools of porpoise. This feeding activity can be spotted from several miles, first by spotting porpoise jumping out of the water. As the boat nears the feeding activity, the splashes of porpoise and tuna will be evident and your heart rate of the angler should go up another twenty beats per minute. To me, the the most exciting aspect of fishing yellowfin tuna is when you can see fish jumping and crashing bait on the surface. Tuna will literally form into a tight swimming fence, much like a living net, all in the attempt to herd the baitfish to the surface. Tuna can be seen jumping over each other in an attempt to get to the food first. Big schools, feeding in this fashion, sound like an approaching rapid on a river, there are so many fish leaping and slashing while trying to feed their voracious appetites.

The job of the Captain is to position the boat in front of an approaching school of feeding tuna. Care must be taken not to approach too fast and put the school down. I have witnessed this too many times when aggressive boat handling ruins the action for everyone. The action can be frantic as the school shifts direction constantly, so you must be ready when the shot presents itself. The cast is made and the fly retrieved as quickly as a double-handed retrieve or scissor strip allows. Generally, the Captain will keep the boat moving to keep in front of the fast moving schools until the anglers hook up. Surface poppers can be quite effective in these situations as long as the retrieve keeps the fly moving fast. I like to switch to an intermediate line as an aid to picking the line quickly off the water and representing it. These techniques work well for tuna, skipjack and bonito.

The Tackle

Rods

Twelve weight and larger rods are recommended if you are serious about tuna. This is a species where the rod choice is definitely tilted toward the lifting rod rather than the sweet casting rod. In our business, the favorite rod is the TFO Blue Water Light for small tuna, and the medium-weight stick for bigger fish, or if you are doubtful as to the size of the fish. I have caught a lot of small tuna (footballs) on ten weight rods. If you can be absolutely certain that nothing larger is lurking in the depths, the ten is a fun football-sized tuna rod. The thing is, that the bait fish that attract the small tuna are also the dinner bell for gorilla-sized tuna, sailfish, large dorado and a host of other tackle busters. My suggestion is to go prepared with the big rods on tuna or bring plenty of spare ten weights.

Reels

I recommend large arbor, direct drives loaded with 300 yards of 30 lb. backing.

Lines

I suggest shooting heads or full-length integrated sinking lines in 400 grains to 800 grains to get most of the action. An intermediate line has its place when chasing breezing tuna that are moving at mach speed on the surface. In these situations there is a slight advantage to the intermediate line where a quick pick up of the fly is necessary. This is especially true for the angler new to handling the fast sinking heads who may have trouble while trying to quickly pick the line up off the water.

Leaders

For most situations on tuna, the presentation is deep, so leaders should be kept to six feet or less. A simple tuna leader can be built with an 18 to 24 inch butt of 40 lb. Jin Kai, looped on both ends and attached to a 16 or 20 lb. class tippet that is 2 to 3 feet long. I do like ferruled leader for the butt section, especially for tuna. They can sprint away from the boat so fast and break knots quicker than about any fish we deal with. Tuna are reputed to be leader shy so I tend not to use a heavy bite tippet if any at all. Since so many tuna are taken on the dead drop, I think the visibility of the leader to the fish is of no less importance than the dampening effect that thick, stiff material has on the action of the fly.

Flies

The Clouser reigns supreme for catching tuna on the dead drop as well as in situations that call for a fast surface retrieve. A good color combination is white body with lots of pear flash, topped with pink, followed by chartreuse and topped with dark blue or purple. For dead drop situations, I fish smaller than the apparent bait as a rule, so flies 2 inches long tied on stout #1 to 1/0 hooks are about right. As a rule,

I imitate the actual size of the bait fish when tuna breezing on the surface around porpoise and dolphins and go smaller than the baitfish when fishing a dead drop. The Mosca Magic has caught a lot of tuna on the surface as does the BBD, Sea Habits and deceiver-style flies. Poppers and crease flies are also effective for tuna working with porpoise or dolphins.

Photograph by Adam Graham

11

Billfish:
Teamwork and Teasing

For a relatively small group of saltwater fly fishermen, billfish are the ultimate challenge on the fly rod. For some, the pursuit is nothing less than an obsession. I had a client for a number of years who was interested in only catching blue marlin on the fly and would not cast to a striped marlin or sailfish. He was one focused individual. Billfish can do that to some people.

This chapter will focus on the two most commonly sought after Pacific species, the sailfish and striped marlin. Blue and black marlin are found along the tropical Pacific coast, but finding one small enough for fly tackle is tough.

Striped marlin and sailfish are within the size range suitable to fly tackle and can be found in larger concentrations.

Sailfish are the most commonly caught billfish on fly. They are plentiful, from the Tropic of Cancer to the Tropic of Capricorn. They are not as tolerant to cooler waters as is the striped marlin and only visit the extreme ends of their range on a short seasonal basis. Central America, and especially Guatemala, is "Sailfish Central" with large concentrations of fish during the winter months. Further north, sails arrive in the Sea of Cortez when the water temperatures top 80 degrees, usually in June.

Striped marlin range further than the sails and have been caught as far north as the Washington coast during El Nino years. They are fairly common in Southern California waters and down the Pacific side of the Baja Peninsula.

Large concentrations of striped marlin congregate in the fall on the Thetis and Potato Banks off-shore from Magdalena Bay on the Baja. These same fish concentrate around the Cape and into the Sea of Cortez later in the fall as the Pacific waters cool. The Sea of Cortez South of la Paz holds fish year round and is one of the best places in the world to experience striped marlin on fly.

The Tackle

The pursuit of billfish is a specialized endeavor and the tackle used is no less so. Stout rods, reels with high capacity lines designed to turn over large flies at close range, are required to ensure any measure of success in landing one of these magnificent creatures.

Rods

The growing popularity of blue water fly fishing has spawned a whole segment of the fly tackle industry to meet the specific needs of the sport. The manufactures have responded by developing rods built for the pursuit of billfish and are designed to lift and fight large fish. A "billfish rod" is a common term used to describe this general group of sticks. The lightest practical rod in the billfish category is the twelve weight. It will handle the smaller sailfish and striped marlin. The Temple Fork Blue Water Light fits into this category.

A more appropriate range of rods encompasses the thirteen through fifteen weights. These rods will handle all but the largest sailfish and most striped marlin as well. In the Blue Water series, this corresponds to the Medium weight rod. The sixteen and seventeen weight rods are designed for the larger striped marlin as well as the blue and black marlin. The Temple Fork equivalent is the Blue Water Heavyweight.

Reels

Large capacity reels with smooth and strong drags are a prerequisite. In the case of billfish, the larger the arbor the better, giving you the best retrieve rate possible. Billfish can change direction radically throwing slack into the line. A slack line often results in the hook coming out and a lost fish. The act of the boat backing down on the fish only amplifies the possibility of slack line.

Spool capacity is also critical when in pursuit of billfish. Reels loaded with four hundred yards of backing are adequate for sails common the Sea of Cortez and smaller striped marlin. If your intent is to seek out billfish exceeding 150 pounds then I would consider a reel capable of holding at least 500 yards of fifty or eighty pound spectra backing.

The Tactics

With few exceptions, catching billfish is all about bait and switch. A variety of teasing styles have evolved varying by region. The Captains in the Sea of Cortez are quite fond of using hook-less, plastic-skirted marlin lures along with one large teaser attached short to a stern cleat. In recent years, I have noticed a few more Captains using at least one bridled bait or a sewn ballyhoo in the teaser spread. In Central American waters, the ballyhoo and sewn fish belly baits are quite common and are usually run in combination with plastic lures and a large teaser. Birds, daisy chains and spreader bar sets are favored in some places as well. The variety of methods and configuration of lures used to attract the fish can become a far greater production than the actual act of casting a fly to billfish. For some this is a turn off, for others it is an exciting multidimensional game.

After running the gamut of teaser spreads, I have come back to a "simple is better" approach. Large and complex spreads may raise more fish, but that doesn't always equate to fish hooked. Skill of deckhands and team work is huge in how many teasers can be trolled and especially pulled from the water when a fish enters the pattern. Deck space and boat design are also factors in deciding how many teasers to run and where to place them. I keep in mind what an older Captain once told me, "The boat is the biggest teaser out there." Regardless of what we drag behind, the prop wash of the boat in the end is really the thing that pulls the fish in.

In the East Cape region and in parts of Central America the Panga-style boat is quite common. Pangas range in size from 21-foot, tiller-driven to 25-foot, center consoles. While being a sound, off shore craft, they lack room and a flying bridge to operate from. Given these restrictions, the spread must be kept simple. A typical configuration is one 11 inch hook-less lure on an out rigger opposite the side of the boat that the fisherman will cast from, since we don't want the back cast to tangle in the outrigger line. The line is let out 'til the lure is riding the front side of the fourth wake behind the boat. On flat, calm days under a high sun, we may drop back to the fifth boat wake. Costa Rican Captains seem to prefer the fifth or sixth wake. When the sun is high and the fish are shy, I tend to agree. When the fish are aggressive, shorter lines behind the boat are better.

My second teaser is a large chum tube with a skirt. This is a homemade affair first shown to me by Mark Dougherty of Baja's Big Game Guide Service and is constructed out of PVC pipe capped at both ends, skirted, painted and drilled with holes. The tube is filled with mashed sardina, squid or chunked skipjack. The teaser is placed on a 25 foot parachute chord plus six feet of 600 pound leader on the stern corner cleat on the same side of the Panga as the out rigger. This doesn't spread the teasers out as I would prefer, but given the room to move quickly in, this approach eliminates the problem of trying to pull the teaser line while essentially in the lap of the caster.

On some days, two lures are all that is need to raise fish and given the small space in which to maneuver, this is simple efficiency at least. In order to hold fish around the boat after the teasers are pulled, I like to have handy a rod rigged with either live or dead bait. This rig can be thrown into the water after the teasers are pulled either before or after the boat is thrown into neutral, depending on the aggressiveness of the fish. A sewn belly on a jig head, a sewn ballyhoo, bridled skipjack or a live mullet all work to hold the interest of a billfish in the set. Striped marlins are prone to hit and run, especially after the boat is put into neutral. These rigs can also be added to the trolling set as an additional line or to replace the skirted jig. As an additional line, I like to place them on a rod holder at the center of the stern. In many cases this will be the rig that the fish will follow to the boat. This is about the limit of what most small crews working in a tight space can handle without the whole experience turning into a cluster.

Cabin cruisers in the 28-foot class and above offer more options. The decks are wider and can accommodate the caster, two working deckhands, plus the Captain on the bridge. The Captain, being higher above the deck is in a good position to see through the glare and better gage the behavior and movement of the fish. Given the additional space and helping hands I like to start with a three teaser set with a sewn-or live-bait rod ready as a throw back. Teaser number one is placed on the out rigger opposite the side of the fisherman, just as we do on the Panga. The second teaser goes on a rod in the corner of the stern the same side as the outrigger and pulled on the third wake behind the boat. The big chum tube goes on the corner cleat on the same side as the fisherman. A rod rigged with a live or sewn bait, is placed at the ready in the rod holder at the center of the transom. If needed, an additional line can be added from the bridge and handled by the captain. This lure is usually set as far back as the sixth or even seventh wake. A skipping lure works best on the long line as it is the most visible from a distance to the boat and easier to track.

The above described sets are starting points in the complex game of tease and switch, and reading fish behavior is the critical ingredient to adjustment and success. If the chum tube doesn't seem to be drawing fish, a bowling pin, daisy chain or other large teasers can be used. Be aware that large daisy chains, especially those on a spreader bar can be hard to pull quickly from the water.

Stage One Teasing

So much rides on the ability to read fish behavior in the act of teasing. Pull the teaser too fast and the fish may lose interest and leave. React too slow and the fish may grab the teaser and leave after detecting the fraud. I have come around to applying the feeding stage approach we use on big roosterfish to fishing for billfish. And like roosterfish, the stages of feeding apply more to the teasing side of the process rather than the presentation of the fly.

A stage-one fish appears as a dark form behind a teaser, displaying a consistent swimming motion. They do not probe with their bills and are not usually lit up. They may pass to another teaser in the set, and if nothing trips their switch, they leave. Stage-one billfish seldom stay long once their curiosity has been satisfied, nor do they often return when we circle the boat back around.

When the fish are reacting in this manner, the first change to the pattern is to drop the out rigger held teaser to the next wake back. When fish are indicating stage-one behavior, the throw back rod is rigged preferably with a live bait and should be thrown quickly to the fish before they decide to drift off. In this case, the bait is also teased longer in front of the fish in the attempt to excite them. Live bait such as mullet are ideal as they tend to stay on the surface where they can be seen swimming by the fisherman and crew doing the teasing. Trying to tease when neither the bait nor fish is visible can be very tough.

In the case of a stage-one fish, the Captain slows the boat, while the deckhand casts the live bait into the water. The bait is allowed to swim behind the boat while carefully monitoring the movement of the fish. The bait stays in the water until the bill shows protruding from behind the bait and then is pulled at the same time the boat is put in neutral and the fly is presented to the fish. Live bait get the greatest reaction from all fish and are especially more effective to fish showing stage-one feeding behavior. There is a trade off in that live bait is harder to control, especially when they see a billfish bearing down on them, and therefore harder to keep in position for the fly caster. If live bait is not available, a dead ballyhoo or fish belly may hold the interest of the stage-one fish.

A sewn dead bait may replace a plastic jig or be added as a third line. Normally this line is set shorter than the lure on the outrigger, typically on the third wake.

Occasionally, free swimming chum thrown in the water will excite a fish enough to take a fly. When this happens, things can get pretty exciting for the fly fisherman. Sails and striped marlin often swim in packs, and live bait can hold fish around the boat long enough to make a cast, just as we do when fishing for dorado. For this purpose, I keep a back-up fly rod rigged for billfish with a sardina or mullet-style fly tied to the end of the billfish leader. This same rig can be used for fish working a bait ball or the surface sleepers we often encounter.

Stage Two Teasing

Typical stage-two fish approaches the lures quickly. They are lit up with their bill wagging behind the teaser ready to strike. Their swimming motion is erratic with sudden spurts of speed as they approach the teaser. Stage-two fish follow the teasers, though usually without striking. With this level of aggression displayed, the other teasers are pulled quickly, leaving the lure the fish is following in the water. This teaser is retrieved just fast enough to stay ahead of the fish until it is in range of the fly caster. At this point I like to seal the deal by throwing a dead bait into the water. Once the fish reacts to the bait, it too is pulled from the water. Leaving the bait in the water too long with a more aggressive fish encourages them to stay on the bait and ignore the fly. Also, the longer the bait is in the water the greater the chance that the fish will grab and pull the bait free and leave. The purpose of presenting the bait is to keep the fish excited, swimming near the boat looking for its food.

Stage Three Teasing

A stage-three fish announces itself immediately with an aggressive attitude, ready to eat. Quite often the first indication of a fish's presence is an all-out attack on the teaser. The bill is clearly visible batting the teaser, and the probing action is then often followed by a vicious strike. Many is the time I have had to pull the teaser from the fish's mouth, then reel like crazy to keep the fish from eating it again. An aggressive fish may quickly switch its attention to another teaser, especially if the first teaser is jerked from its grasp. The pace of pulling the teasers is fast, followed by a quick presentation of the fly, especially if the fish has had a hard lure in its mouth.

If the billfish has repeatedly batted the teaser with its bill, the best presentation of the fly is a dead drop imitation of a wounded bait fish. Few marlin or sails can resist the soft-settling motion of a slowly sinking fly. A dead bait can be used to hold the fish close to the boat, but care must be used in how long it is left out there. A true stage-three fish is extremely aggressive and will quickly pounce on the bait and quite possibly grab it before it can be snatched away.

Getting the Hookup

The fish is now appropriately lit up and ready to eat the fly. The teasers (and especially the baited teasers) are out of the water and the boat is in neutral. It is now up to the fly fisher to make the presentation. To ensure that the presentation goes well, a little pre-work and preparation is in order. The whole crew should run some practice drills beforehand simulating the approach of a fish, including the pulling of teasers, boat in neutral and the actual presentation of the fly. The best cure for buck fever is practiced, familiarity with the process, Many have learned the hard way on this.

A number of years ago, my partner Larry and I had a day off from guiding and decided to take the opportunity to go fishing for billfish, a rare treat for us working guides. We trolled all day without a fish in the teasers until late in the day when an aggressive marlin went on the attack. I was on the fly rod and Larry held the teasing rod. When the moment of truth came, I jumped the gun on the cast, not waiting till the teaser was clear and made the perfect wing shot on the teaser, nailing it in mid air with the fly. Everything fell in a heap back into the water. Larry and I frantically tried to untangle fly from teaser while the marlin continued to attack what had now become a combo meal. By the time we got tangled lines sorted, the fish had abandoned his effort and swam off looking for a tamer meal. Afterwards, little was said between us for several miles of travel on a calm sea.

Take care to coil the right amount of fly line into a bucket and hang the fly in such a way as not to get caught on anything as it is tossed into the water. The drill is to toss or flip the fly onto the first wave wake behind the boat once the fish is spotted in the teasers. The pull of the boat on the fly loads the rod in preparation of the cast. The fly is kept there out of immediate view of the fish till the teaser is pulled and the boat thrown into neutral. At this point, make a strong single back cast to get the fly moving in the air, then come forward with a wide loop. The best cast should fall behind and to the side of the fish. This forces the fish to turn and take the fly sideways, resulting in a greater chance for a solid hook up. The fly taken this way will also be in a better position for the boat to follow the fish. The Captain will wants to keep the boat on the side of the fish that it is hooked on.

Once the fly is in the water, no stripping motion is required initially as the boat will still be moving even after it is thrown into neutral. As the boat comes to a halt, a long, steady pull can be imparted on the fly. The take is sudden and savage, but you must keep your cool and set the hook only after the fish is turned and headed a way from the boat.

The object is to set when the hooks will catch in the corner of the mouth. Too quick a set may end up with the hook in the roof of the mouth or into the bill. In most cases a poor hook set will pop out on the first jump, or anytime that slack occurs in the line.

Placing the rod tip under the water while the fish is moving off prior to the hook set helps to position the fly in the corner of the mouth due to water pressure running against the thick fly line. This rod maneuver aids the hook set on both J-hooks and circle hooks. Flies tied on J-hooks still require that the angler aggressively strip strike the fish after it turns away from the boat, while water pressure holds the hook, leader and line in good alignment to the corner of the mouth. Circle hooks merely require that the line comes tight while smoothly lifting the rod against the water pressure on the fly line. In either case when the fish feels the hook stick they will explode into a blistering run. At this point, the rod should be held at a slight angle away from the fish while allowing it to run against the reel. Touching the rim of the reel at this point will most likely result in an immediate break off. Be patient and enjoy the show, your work has just begun.

Laid Up Fish

Billfish are commonly encountered loafing or swimming along on the surface and present a unique opportunity for the fly fisherman. In the past, we used to circle the boat around these fish with the hope that they would engage with the trolled teasers. An approach I favor now is to quietly drift up on the fish and toss a live bait in the water about twenty feet off their nose. When the fish responds to the teaser, it is pulled out of the water and replaced with the fly which is thrown right on top of the excited billfish. Many sleeping billfish are not interested in food and will simply drift off. The ones who do react to teaser and fly can leave a lasting memory of an explosive strike. An alternative to this approach is to throw a large hook-less popper to the fish and hope for a reaction and follow, much as we work teasers to roosterfish.

The pursuit of billfish is a highly specialized enterprise in terms of tackle and tactics. In all aspects of saltwater fishing, preparation is important. In the case of billfish, it is paramount. The slightest imperfection in line connections, leader knots, reel drag system and rod can spell failure. Billfish on the fly is a team work affair that not only requires good equipment, leaders and knots, but the development and execution of a good tactical plan. The plan needs to be understood and agreed to by Captain, deckhands and fly fisherman. In between the plan and execution come preparation and practice. A few dry runs will insure that everyone understands their part and timing. Practice and familiarity goes a long way to settle nerves and better manage Buck Fever. In war they say that the best plan is good 'til the first shot is fired, and after that it is all improvisation. The same can be said of trying to hook a hundred plus pound billfish on the fly. Regardless of the plan, every fish is different in its aggression, pace of attack, preference to teasers, level of excitement and willingness to hang by the boat. A good plan, going in that is practiced and understood, provides a foundation from which to improvise. To do otherwise is to invite utter chaos on the deck.

Photograph by Brian O'Keefe

Photograph by Brian O'Keefe

Conclusion

Writing *Fly Fishing the Baja and Beyond* has been a five year odyssey culminating from thirty years of exploring the Baja Peninsula, fishing the waters of the Pacific and Sea Of Cortez. Thirteen of those years have been spent guiding clients on Pangas, cruisers, kayaks and pounding the beach for roosters. It is from the perspective of a working guide that I approached the creation of this book. As much as I love to fish, and I have learned greatly from my angling experience, the lessons learned while guiding offer a different viewpoint from which to observe the feeding behavior of the fish and their reaction to the presentation of the fly.

The fly fishing community entered the territory of applied behavior on the trout stream in the '60s and '70s when aquatic entomology and observed fish feeding behavior merged into a more effective and consistent way to catch trout on fly. The ability to observe and interpret fish feeding behavior has been key in terms of a more consistent approach to catching saltwater species as well. Understanding fish feeding behavior is an important first step in solving the fish catching puzzle. Tackle choices, fly selection and tactical approach are all interconnected to understanding the feeding behavior of the targeted species. Aggressive fish are relatively easy to figure out with a wide variety of flies and presentations paying off in hooked fish. The caution, expressed here, is the tendency to interpret this snap shot in the feeding life of a fish and then apply the technique to all circumstances. The curious non-feeder is a fish of false hope, giving what appears to be a real interest in your presentation when in reality they are just not aggressive to the point of eating an artificial. This is a hard pill for the angler to swallow and in its own way leads us to misinformed conclusions. It is the feeding behavior in the middle that I have found to be the most enlightening in terms of developing a consistent approach. The fish that is hungry but still cautious will take the fly if certain trigger mechanisms are pulled. While these techniques probably won't change the curious non feeder into a feeder, the tactics will work for the cautious to very aggressive feeders.

Developing the ability to differentiate between fish that follow, then refuse and those that eat the fly is a first important step in gaining consistent tactical approaches. Here again as the observant guide I have been able to see subtle differences in fish swimming attitude and reaction to the fly I tended to miss when I was totally immersed in my attempt to catch the fish. A very common reaction from my clients to this day when a fish refuses is for them to say "He missed it," or "Damn it, I pulled it right out of his mouth!" When in reality I saw the change in the fishes swimming attitude the moment the fly paused between strips or the mouth close just before turning off the fly. In many cases the swimming pattern indicated curiosity with no intention of taking the fly. Without an understanding of feeding behavior and an interpretation of what just happened, the tendency is to then slow the retrieve down, even stop the fly in front of the next twenty or so fish encountered. After all, the misinterpretation was that the fly was pulled out of its mouth or the fish missed the fly because it was moving too fast. Ironically, the really aggressive fish can come along and eat the slower retrieve and then you go along for a long time thinking that you now have roosterfish figured out.

Understanding fish feeding behavior and recognizing the difference in responses to presentation will take us in the other direction in that the refusal came because the fly didn't act like normal prey and was thus rejected. The trigger mechanism then becomes one of pulling the fly away from the fish, as a mullet or sardina would do to escape, in order to get the fish to eat. By the way, the super aggressive fish would have most likely taken the fly on a faster retrieve as well.

This whole idea of pulling the fly away from fish makes logical sense, but is difficult at times for us to implement.

For me the learning process is continuous. Each fishing day, each fishing season provides new lessons learned. This book took five years in creation due in part to a busy guide schedule, but also because of the continuing learning process. I would finish a guide season and return to the book only to tweak or re-write with new insights chapters I considered completed.

The learning process has been exiting, some times frustrating and ultimately rewarding. I have much yet to learn and I enjoy the prospects of that process. I don't pretend to have all the answers. I do feel comfortable that I may be starting to ask the right questions.

I hope that you have found this work interesting, informative and entertaining, perhaps in places controversial and thought provoking. Saltwater fly fishing opens new doors for the long rod fisher, new species, new tactics, and new adventures. The Sea of Cortez and the Pacific beyond is a great place to get initiated.

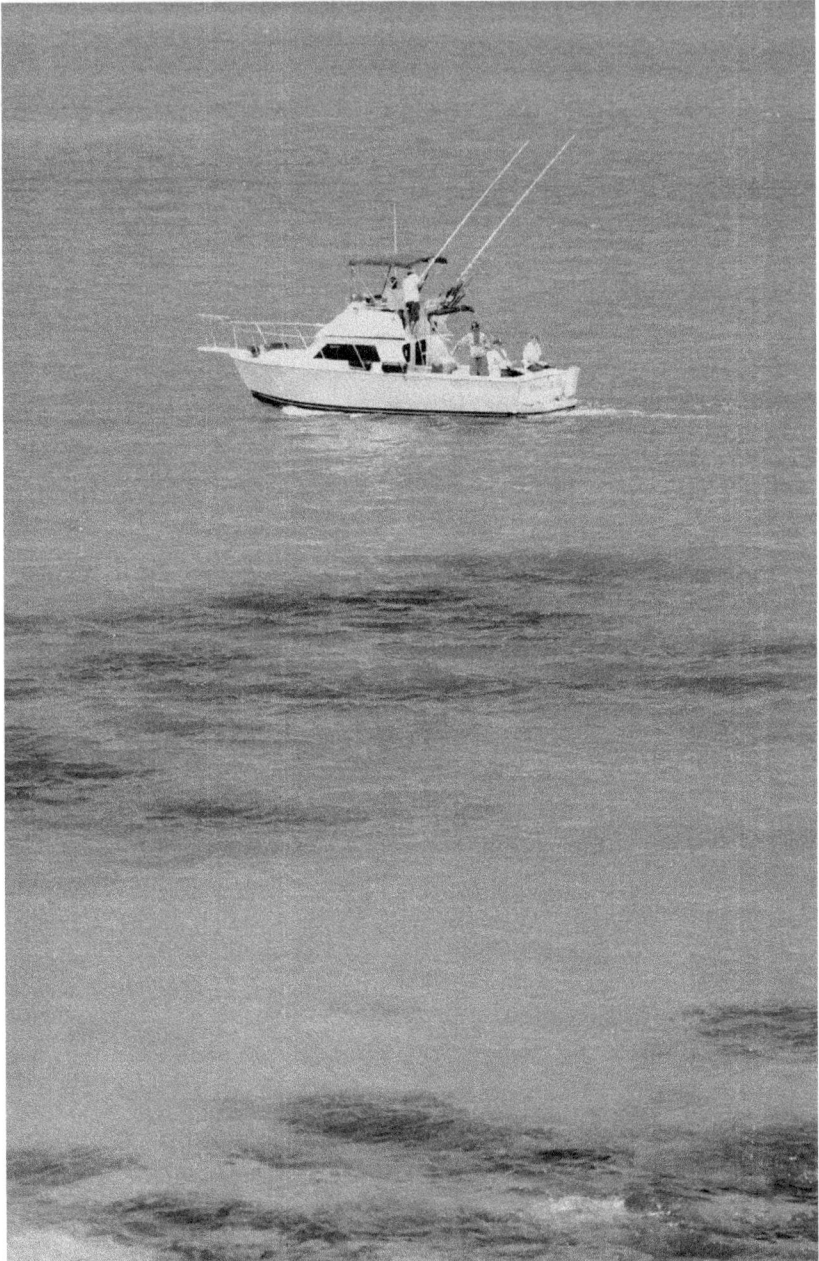

Photograph by Brian O'Keefe

Index

Mike Rieser's outfitter guide experience dates back to 1974. Mike operates the fly fishing/light tackle guide service for the Van Wormer Resorts on the East Cape of Baja Sur.

Robert Van Wormer

1925 – 2010

Descanse en Paz
A Baja Legend

www.ingramcontent.com/pod-product-compliance
Lightning Source LLC
Chambersburg PA
CBHW031302090426
42742CB00007B/559